TWINSBURG LIBRARY
TWINSBURG OHIO

Start-Up Smart

How to start and build a successful business
on a budget

D0325218

by Robin Bennett

$
Start-up
658.11
Ben

www.startupsmart.co.uk

HARRIMAN HOUSE LTD

3A Penns Road
Petersfield
Hampshire
GU32 2EW
GREAT BRITAIN

Tel: +44 (0)1730 233870
Fax: +44 (0)1730 233880
Email: enquiries@harriman-house.com
Website: www.harriman-house.com

First published in Great Britain in 2010
Copyright © Harriman House Ltd

The right of Robin Bennett to be identified as Author has been asserted in accordance
with the Copyright, Design and Patents Act 1988.

Set in Palatino and Eurostile

ISBN: 978-1906659-83-7

British Library Cataloguing in Publication Data
A CIP catalogue record for this book can be obtained from the British Library.

All rights reserved; no part of this publication may be reproduced, stored in a retrieval
system, or transmitted in any form or by any means, electronic, mechanical,
photocopying, recording, or otherwise without the prior written permission of the
Publisher. This book may not be lent, resold, hired out or otherwise disposed of
by way of trade in any form of binding or cover other than that in which it is published
without the prior written consent of the Publisher.

Printed and bound in Great Britain by CPI Antony Rowe, Chippenham.

No responsibility for loss occasioned to any person or corporate body acting or refraining
to act as a result of reading material in this book can be accepted by the Publisher or by
the Author.

Start-Up Smart

Hh Harriman House

Harriman House is one of the UK's leading independent publishers of financial and business books. Our catalogue covers personal finance, stock market investing and trading, current affairs, business and economics. For more details go to: www.harriman-house.com

Contents

Preface

First up, this book will not make you a million inside of three months – nor will it make any other wildly optimistic claims such as saving the world, fundamentally changing the way we think about business or improving your chances of pulling.

This book is a detailed description of how to start a small business from scratch, with relatively little money, and how that business can give you a comfortable standard of living with little or no risk in the long term. No more and no less.

The advice contained in these pages is based on what I have found to work over the last 20-odd years in business.

About Me

I founded the Bennett Group in 1992 shortly after leaving London University with a slightly dubious degree in Modern Languages.

Whilst at university, to keep me in cheap red wine and cigarettes, I started a sandwich business. When I finally graduated – not having a burning desire to be an entrepreneur – I put on a pair of brogues and prepared for life as a cavalry officer. By mutual consent, my commanding-officer-to-be, the Queen (presumably), and I decided that Her Majesty's forces weren't the best place for my talents. I then put on a pair of Doc Martens and became a grave digger in East Sheen, followed by a stint selling aerial pictures of people's houses door-to-door in Yorkshire.

After about eight months, I finally landed a 'proper' job working as the business manager for a music magazine in Soho and got to meet a lot of semi-famous people. However, this might have been good life experience but I had the distinct feeling after a year that it was getting me nowhere fast. So I left.

The UK was in the middle of its last recession and, as was the case at the time of writing, banks were very sceptical about lending to anyone without a track record or indeed any of their own cash. £3000 was the most that any bank would lend at the time without security and so, thanks in part to a good business plan, the Bennett Group was set up using just a modest loan of that amount from Barclays Bank. It has grown fairly steadily since, without resorting to large-scale or irresponsible borrowing. It now operates in the UK, USA, France, Germany, Hong Kong and Australia.

Happily each part of the group continues to be profitable, thriving on the principle that fair pricing and fair play will always find a solid market. Crucially, all have been started for less than £5000. The smallest (dog-sitting) cost £50 to set up and made £15,000 profit in its first year; the largest – Aktuel Translations – has fared reasonably well and was even recognised in *Who's Who* as one of the fastest growing UK companies of 2003.

The Bennett Group

1992:   London Tutors. Home tuition and supply teaching.

1993:   The Aktuel Translation Group. Technical translation.

1999:   Y2K translations. Translation for the publishing industry, renamed Quarto Translations in January 2006.

2002:   ExpressTranslators.com. Online translation service 24/7.

2003:   Monster Books. Self-published children's poetry and illustrated books.

2003:   Bennett Investments. Investment advice.

2005: Patent Translations International. Patent translation.

2005: Comp Farm Kennels. Dog-sitting on an Oxfordshire farm.

2009: River. Consultancy for companies spending over £2 million per annum on translation.

2010: Thisisplanetearth.com. Website collecting the best articles from around the world.

1.

Planning for Getting Started

In which we ponder on just what we are getting ourselves into and then set about getting the money to make it all possible.

Basic Strategies

- You do not have to be radical. The soundest business ideas are rarely the most original, and regularly the ones that you know from everyday experience work well.

- Likewise a USP (Unique Selling Point) does not have to be excessively unique. Often it can be something as simple as good service, slightly lower prices or local appeal.

- If other people can make a similar business work, then so can you – usually if you want it enough.

- Keep it simple. Make sure that the business idea is one that you can easily explain in less than 100 words. This is critical – if you get in a muddle now, it doesn't bode well.

- Do your own business plan; it will be your best opportunity to really scrutinise the strengths and weaknesses of your idea.

- Choose your source of funding very carefully. Rank them according to cost and timescales of repayment. For example, grants are best, credit cards are worst.

- All business sectors have their own set of rules – insider dos and don'ts, if you like. Find out what these are before starting. The best places are usually online forums and industry networking events.

Defining Your Goals

Like I said, this is not a get-rich quick book. If you like, take this opportunity to thumb forward to the Appendix, look at the Cash Flow Forecast and decide whether the sort of figures I am outlining as an achievable goal in the first and second years are your cup of tea.

When all's said and done, the next 115 pages describe how £5000, judiciously acquired and spent, should allow for a £35,000-£50,000 salary in the first year and anything between £100,000 and £200,000 thereafter. I am prepared to admit that this might not be enough for some, and I have a feeling that there are quite a few people out there who would scorn such an obvious lack of ambition. And, to an extent, I'd go along with that. Like anybody, there are days when I do wonder what it would be like to be stupendously rich, own an island somewhere and have footmen. Some people that I know – people I'd even call close friends – have annual salaries topping seven figures and there's nothing morally wrong with that. They work hard, they have friends, love their family, pat dogs... etc. However, I usually make myself feel better by remembering that, statistically speaking, it's highly unlikely that the vast majority of us will ever be able to achieve great wealth, either by chance, hard grind or stealth.

I'll quantify that by saying that, according to the *Sunday Times* Rich List, there are actually fewer than 3000 cash millionaires living in the British Isles today (a mere 0.015% of the working population). Yet sales of 'how to make millions' books and CDs, not to mention the weekend seminars and online courses, must outstrip that figure

1000 to one. And there's a reason for this – I suspect, because it takes determination, luck and perhaps ruthlessness to achieve great wealth, that most people, in their hearts, don't consider this a realistic lifestyle choice: they say to themselves 'I'm not prepared to give myself grief over an aim that it is statistically unlikely I'll ever achieve'.

On the other hand, according to the Office for National Statistics there are 1.3 million individuals (out of a working population of just over 20 million) from all sorts of backgrounds who quietly get on with their lives whilst earning over six figures. They may not be deliriously happy all the time but, according to the 2008 British Household Panel Survey (BHPS), people living in middle- to high-income areas really do seem to be happier than most of us, most of the time. Crucially, though, this list excludes stupendously high earners in hotspots such as parts of Surrey and Central London who are statistically almost as miserable as the Scots.

Nearly 1.5 people out of 20 *are* odds I can live with.

So, if not incalculable riches and debauched weekends bobbing about on big private yachts with the rich and the political, the first thing to sort out when going into business for yourself is what you actually want to get out of it.

For myself, I realised that I simply didn't like working for someone else. I found it stressful worrying about a future (*my* future) that was essentially in someone else's hands (my boss's). By the time I started my business, I'd only been out of university for around a year but I had the conviction that other people's problems and the expectations they had of me sorting these problems out their way, were always going to be a lot less fulfilling than sorting out my own problems in my own way.

Funnily enough, at the time I seemed to have the dream graduate job – given we were in the grip of the last real recession. I'd given up the grave digging and the door-to-door sales and was now working as business manager of a music magazine for one of the

most colourful entrepreneurs England has produced in recent years
– Peter Boizot, founder of The Pizza Express Group and many other
ongoing concerns. What most impressed me at the time about Mr
Boizot MBE was his ability to combine his interests (namely eating,
drinking, music and sport), with his business activities (namely,
Pizza Express, Peroni Beer, The Soho Jazz Festival, *Jazz Express
Magazine*, sponsorship of the National Hockey league, and lately
ownership of Peterborough United FC).

I was 22 when I started and absurdly green, in many respects, for
the job in hand. My remit was broadly to ensure his activities
outside pizzas (mainly in jazz, blues and publishing) were as
profitable as possible. The delegation of trust and responsibility is
not only one of the marks of a leader but also of someone who has
deep pockets, because I inevitably made stupid mistakes that cost
him money. I also managed to stretch his patience to breaking point
on a number of occasions.

In fact his great strength lay in bringing out the best in people, in
spite of their failings. Tick-box company culture, whereby the
ultimate employee is measured on a set of criteria drafted by
someone in HR, doesn't usually work, because the perfect
employee doesn't actually exist. Also, people who care about what
boxes are being ticked don't usually have their mind on the actual
job.

Staff who were taken on by Peter very rarely ended up doing what
they were actually hired for after a few months. Instead their role
was often amended to something that a) they were good at and, b)
they cared about.

I've seen the same thing work in other places. The best maths
teacher I ever had was previously the head gardener at the school;
he had been asked to sit in on a class to cover staff shortages during
a flu epidemic. I'm not sure what possessed him to take it upon
himself to spend the next 40 minutes teaching us, instead of
allowing the class to drill holes in the desks with our compasses
and stare out of the window until the bell went: however, teach us

he did, and he turned out to be a natural. Not just at maths, either. By the time I left he was teaching history and English and coaching the football team. Similarly; someone I know very well went a step further and employed a sparky and intelligent girl he met at a stag-do who took all her clothes off for a living. Six months later he told me that she'd become one of his most successful salespeople.

In time, I came to realise two important things about the world of business management or entrepreneurship:

Fact one

Entrepreneurship is, for the most part, a thoroughly enjoyable activity. It doesn't matter if, to an outsider, your affairs most probably seem chaotic – you can have as many separate businesses as you like provided they all fulfil a useful function, have a chance of making some money at some point and do not involve the undertaking of activities considered illegal. In fact the more muddled your activities are the better, as then only you know what's going on and this can be its own reward.

Fact two

Commerce is not a mystery, open to few and understood by infinitely less. It's just good common sense and a willingness to get up in the mornings and do what you were talking about doing the night before. This also goes back to what I was saying a couple of paragraphs ago about finding it hard to do things someone else's way. Out of all the really impressive entrepreneurs I have met I have noticed that they all have one thing in common: an uncanny ability to propose the most ludicrous solutions to problems that would turn out to be the best resolution in hindsight. Going back a few years, I put this down to some sort of business extra-sensory perception. With the benefit of just under two decades of running my own show, so to speak, I know this to be perhaps just the impression they want to give. The truth of the matter is that there are many ways to skin a cat and having autonomy over your decisions and good staff allows you to formulate the most eccentric working practices and carry them through (most of the time) with success.

This is a wonderful fact of life and precisely the reason why many successful entrepreneurs and politicians can afford to seem so daft at times.

Keeping this in mind, I set out to achieve the following goals:

- I would never work for someone else again and, in doing so, would never again be subject to someone else's pattern or tempo. This means, quite simply, doing things my own way and in my own time.

- I also wanted to have enough money not to worry about money. A little scorning of the trappings of wealth amongst one's contemporaries is as fashionable as it is rewarding but only if you've got the choice between splashing out or slumming it. It knocks rather hollow to decry the material when you've actually got nothing anyway.

- Again, it sounds shallow, but I wanted to eat in reasonably good restaurants and not worry about who paid the bill or whether to order another bottle of wine or take a cab home. I wanted to be able to choose how I educated my kids and I didn't want success to take more than five years because I wanted to be young enough to enjoy it.

- Likewise, I would have enough money to live where I wanted and take long sabbaticals. I don't want to give you the wrong impression, though. I work fairly hard. Also, real holidays, as many people know, are not possible for me. I carry a mobile wherever I go and it is always switched on. You must be prepared to be constantly available, even if you are not really there. But we do go away as a family a lot, mainly to avoid the English winter, and we do take long weekends to nice hotels with warm pools and towels larger than the ones you have at home.

- I wanted to enjoy myself at work.

I hope all this does not sound too self-satisfied, since the achievement of a comfortable lifestyle is not a very difficult agenda. In fact, financial independence is not as hard as some people imagine and really is achievable in about two to three years with an initial investment of under £5000.

I didn't take the decision to leave the comforts of a regular pay cheque behind too lightly. But the more I thought about it, the less stupid it seemed. Anyway, after another few months of toying with ideas and talking to people, I felt I was ready and I left. With no money in the bank I needed some form of work whilst I set up the business, so I became a gardener for a while and lived on a boat. The daffodils you see sprouting liberally on London's Shepherd's Bush Green south side were entirely my doing.

The time spent messing around with bulbs and a Hammersmith and Fulham Council trowel allowed time for the ever-critical Planning and Preparation.

Planning and Preparation

It's a fact of life that we need to plan. Nearly everyone who starts a business produces a business plan with a cash flow forecast, profit and loss account, etc. This is right and proper but where most businesses fail early on is that their plan is really just a wish list, mostly to justify their decision to leave their job or to satisfy a bank's lending requirement. The real tragedy is that people often take the bogus plan and use it as a blueprint. They end up believing their own fibs and are inevitably dismayed when things do not go the way they expected.

Give things a rose-tinted perspective for potential investors by all means, but make sure you have a realistic plan sitting at home in a prominent place. It is perfectly fair to say that this will be based on your original, 'this is how I would like things to turn out in an ideal world' plan. But starting a small business is multi-tasking in the extreme – so assume that everything will take twice as long and cost twice as much and you'll be roughly near the mark when planning.

I will go through the plan in detail in the following pages but, in theory, a plan should cover the first one to two years and no more for a business from scratch. It is no good looking at it as a purely financial document either. This is because it should lay out as clearly as possible what your business is about and why it will work, what you will do to go about achieving this and quite possibly where others have failed.

Prior to writing the plan set down, in about 100 words, the basic idea behind your business. This is an essential exercise in my view.

Clarity here is crucial because you will be required to explain your business *ad nauseam* to dozens of people with drinks or, better still, cheque books in their hands over the next few weeks, days or even years. These are often important people with a stake in your future, people with influence, money and sometimes – alarmingly – acumen. They will also inevitably be your loved ones, who frankly deserve to know why you've left your stable (if dull) job, sold the car and pawned the cat. They may be potential backers who will want a bloody good reason why they should give you part of their hard-earned wealth and above all, they will ultimately be potential clients. In summary, if someone you need to convince of the value of your idea greets what you have to say about it with any degree of incomprehension, uninterest or – worse still – frank amazement, then what you really should be thinking at this stage is, 'Oh dear'.

Now, if people do look a bit baffled by your idea, you don't necessarily need to give up on the whole project there and then. But you probably do need to go back and refine what you are saying to people.

This always makes me think of the film 'The Hudsucker Proxy'. Tim Robbins plays a fresh-faced hick starting work in a faceless corporation. At the start of the film he is given to showing people a grubby piece of paper upon which he has drawn a circle. Nothing else; just a circle. It's an idea (he proclaims with an evangelic glint in his eye) that will make his career! Of course, no one can make head nor tail of the significance of this circle or what the idea is. Seeing the look on their faces he then says, 'It's for kids!' as if that explains everything. In the end, he finally gets across that it's a hula hoop (the type kids used to spin around their middles, not the more-ish potato snack), everyone in America buys one and his place in history is assured.

I always try at the outset to express the idea in under 30 seconds and if people I try this particular thumbnail sketch on nod and make generally affable noises then I know I am safely onto the next stage.

The Business Plan

A business plan is at least a day's work, far more if research is needed. It sounds dull and not at all entrepreneurial, but it's vital.

If you want to get a loan or an overdraft facility from a bank or sponsor, then you'll need a business plan as a minimum requirement. Secondly, the business plan, and the discipline involved in formulating one, is often an invaluable source of inspiration. Some of my best ideas on top of original, merely OK, ideas come to me whilst going through the plan and writing down what is already in my head.

It's an important thing to remember that many businesses fail in their early days because the director simply runs out of steam. One of the causes of this is that the task of taking nothing and making it into something can seem huge or pointless at different intervals. Planning splits the jobs up into manageable chunks and gives a sense of forward momentum on the days when it seems like nothing is ever going to happen.

A note on your future

The business plan is a good opportunity for some stern reflection with yourself about your idea. If, during the course of writing it you begin to suspect that you might not be able to sell the idea, or sustain an interest in it (a good pointer is when the plan starts to bore even you) or you begin to doubt your ability to run it effectively, then it's time to rethink. A valuable piece of advice, that I never followed, is to do the plan before you've taken steps to leave your job.

Presentation and contents

A small point but nevertheless an important one, is always to make sure you use decent quality paper for your business plan and put it in a properly bound folder. Photocopied paper, stapled together, is not going to get you far. Gimmicks, like cartoons, laminations, etc do actually work, provided what's inside is an impeccably argued document.

A good business plan must have a contents and an index, clearly laying out the following elements as a minimum requirement:

- executive summary
- market overview
- objectives and strategy
- *modus operandi*

- structure

- schedules

- cash flow forecast and notes

- appendices.

Executive summary

This is the attention grabber. It operates on very much the same principle I talked about earlier, in that you have to be able to explain and, ideally, sell your business idea in just a few pithy sentences.

This should take one short-ish paragraph. The next paragraph in should outline what you are looking for in terms of capital and what growth you are expecting in one to two years.

Any investor will scan the executive summary to see whether they are going to waste their precious time reading any more of your plan, so it goes without saying that it's important to get it right.

Market overview

Part overview of the market you plan to operate in, part justification for why it needs another operator (namely, you).

A really good description of the market should answer the second question without any subjective comments from you. For example, a proposal to mount a meat importing operation to supply butchers in the North of England should show data that suggests there is a market there and that you will have little or no local competition. Really good statistics speak eloquently enough without you having to labour the point of why you have decided to open for business.

Again, you are after brevity but the reader needs facts here so don't be afraid of detail where it is:

- relevant

- real.

Facts and figures must come from an independent data source (i.e., don't make them up). Don't fall into the easy error of giving them a history of the market since the Industrial Revolution because you think they might be interested. There must be a point to what you are saying (and I'm not sure they'll be interested in a history lesson).

Always bear in mind that reading other people's business plans is quite boring, especially if you do it a lot. Make it interesting by showing them, as concisely as possible, how easy it will be for you (and them) to make money.

Objectives and strategy

How are you planning on taking advantage of the market place you've just described so eloquently and what strategies are you planning on employing to achieve this?

The first aspect can be answered in a series of bullet points (along the lines of percentage share of the market in two years and expected turnover). Note, this must be backed-up by your cash flow at the end of the plan.

The strategies are an outline of the marketing tactics you will employ to achieve these goals. Again, strategies must be linked to the financial side of the business. Good marketing ideas cost money – so don't boast about a global TV advertising campaign if you are only trying to raise £5K.

Modus operandi

Simply put, how will the business operate? It must address the management of your workflow.

An investor wants to know that you are sufficiently aware of the daily management requirements your business has, from quoting to completion of work.

The modus operandi should show what a sleekly efficient operation you are planning on running. It should describe a business that is the perfect marriage between cost and efficiency. In fact, the reader should get to the end of this section and say to him or herself, 'By Jove, yes, that's exactly how I would run [insert business name]!'

Structure of the business

I know some people who flick straight to here after reading the executive summary. Basically, what they are interested in seeing, before going any further, is who is going to be running things and what qualifies them to do so.

If I had ten pence for every plan I've read that doesn't answer this question properly I could almost afford to go bail out RBS.

So, for example, if you've worked in a video-hire shop for six years since graduating with a BSc in Sociology, then you are going to have your work cut out persuading someone that you are going to launch the next generation of computer networking systems on the flimsy basis that you've seen *The Matrix* 87 times.

If you haven't got a lot of experience, then find someone who has and get them to act in an advisory capacity. You would be amazed at how many people will be flattered by such a request; enough to work for free or at least the very reasonable rate of the occasional slap-up meal.

The other part here is the legal structure. Briefly, your business can be any one of the following:

Sole trader

Description: Just as it sounds. A person trading on their own, i.e. the sole owner of a business (you are allowed staff as a sole trader).

Strengths: You can become a sole trader simply by waking up one morning and announcing, 'I am a sole trader'. So it's all very simple, with no forms to fill out. This is how most people start off. You do need to inform the local tax office, who will make you pay about £5 national insurance on standing order quarterly, regardless of what you earn, and then national insurance again on your profits for the year.

Downside: Perceived as being at the slightly grubby end of the business hierarchy. Even if self-image is not a problem, you might want to consider that banks don't like lending money to sole traders, so it's hard for them to get a loan to buy a box of pens, let alone a mortgage.

Most importantly, however, a sole trader is one and the same as their business. This means that if the business gets sued or goes bust, you could end up losing everything. It's risky, when you consider the other options.

Limited company

Description: A limited company means you are creating another entity separate from yourself, limiting your liability. These days you can purchase a Ltd Co. 'off the shelf' so to speak for around £50 (ex VAT) and have all the documentation sorted in less than a week.

Strengths: Because your company is a separate person, technically as distinct from you as the bloke opposite on the bus, there is less risk of you going down with the ship if things go wrong. In reality, just how badly its downfall affects you really depends on how responsibly you have run the business. It is also (and strangely so, in the light of what I have just said) the respectable option. People will ask if your concern is a limited company and will be pleased if the answer is a positive.

Downside: Some people shy away from the paperwork and legalese, even though these are greatly reduced these days. It costs around £30 a year to file accounts and register with Companies House.

Partnerships

Description: When you go into business with one or more individuals. You can be a sole-trader partnership or a limited-company partnership.

Strengths: You get to share the burdens of responsibility, you have someone to spend your lunchtimes with and when it all goes wrong you can save face by privately putting the blame on each other.

Downside: Obviously, things can get nasty. Make sure that you get the legal stuff right at the outset, including the considerations surrounding the eventuality that one of you may want to leave at some point.

Unfortunately, there is not enough space in this little book for an exhaustive summary of company legal structures, and anyway, I'm not sure you'll need that much detail at this stage. If you are in any doubt, get some professional advice.

Schedules

It is important that you put in a realistic schedule of how the business is going to develop in the short term (the first one to two years is about right).

Again, it's probably a good idea to lay it out as bullet points with notes underneath that explain what you plan to happen at each stage, split into three to six-month chunks. This means the reader can see at a glance what they should expect from you in terms of progress.

Cash flow forecast

The cash flow forecast must show that any loans you have managed to get to start the business should more than cover the start-up period until such time as you start getting some money in from clients and customers.

If they like the executive summary and the breakdown of the personalities involved in the business, the next part a true professional will turn to is the cash flow forecast. What they want to see is the 'bottom line'. So called because it's found at the bottom of the list of figures, and is a total of sales minus expenses – i.e. your profit.

I have included at the back of this book the business plan I used for a joint-venture recruitment consultancy I helped set up a few years ago. By then I was beginning to get it right and this represents my most accurate plan to date. We actually achieved about 10% under the predicted turnover in the first year but the costings and overall progression is right.

What comes first in the forecast, however, are the notes or explanations.

Explain in the notes how you are arriving at sales figures for the business. You cannot make the sales figures up on the basis that this is how you hope things are going to go. You must start with a reasonable premise along the lines of 'One week's sales elicit an average of twenty leads. Research has shown that 5% of leads turn into business, the average contract being worth x amount in terms of turnover.'

If the assumption is credible, then you can work out the progression in your turnover fairly easily. For example, if every client yields £1000 of business on average, and your sales initiative should reasonably expect a four client catch per month, then your business will grow at a rate of £4000 per month, until you can afford to have an extra person selling, in which case turnover will increase by £8000 a month, although don't make the 'rooky' mistake of forgetting that costs will also go up.

This is all fairly on the rosy and simplistic side so factor in loss of clients on a six-monthly basis, in that you will expect to lose 10% of your business each half year through natural wastage. This will show you are taking a realistic view of things.

You might also use the notes to justify certain expenses or explain why you have made certain assumptions.

The cash flow itself should be done in the form of a spread sheet (see the example at the back) and include a month-by-month forecast of income and expenditure. The 'flow' part of the forecast is all about showing what your bank balance is at the beginning of the month and then at the end, when all your income and expenses have actually gone out.

Again, have a rose-tinted forecast set aside for investors and suchlike but make sure you have done at least one worst-case-scenario plan as well – a plan that shows what would happen if you got the minimum amount of investment and higher than expected overheads.

Remember that professionals who read business plans all the time have a rough idea of what each sector of the business world will take for what amount of investment. They also have a really good nose for bullshit. So beware: however convincing you are on paper, you are never going to tell them that a £5000 loan for your loft-fitting partnership is going to generate £10 million turnover in six months.

Appendices

Put anything here that you feel is relevant but would disturb the 'flow' of the plan in the main part: supporting evidence to back up statements made in the market survey, relevant case studies, that sort of thing.

I don't think you should feel the need to pad out the plan with masses of appendices. In all honesty, I doubt they get read that much.

Sources of Investment

There is no mistaking the fact that despite there being over 30 nations in the world with unacceptable levels of poverty there is also a sea of money out there. For example, although the cash pumped into the venture capital industry peaked (so far) in 2000, it still averages out at around US$30 billion being handed out a year. Even in 2008, when frankly almost all banks looked shaky one way or another, UK commercial lending to small businesses stood at just under £50 billion.

Knowing that there is money out there is one thing, getting one's grubby mitts on it is quite something else. I will deal with the most common sources in this section.

Venture capital

This is where a firm of venture capitalists look at your idea on paper, take you out for a nice lunch somewhere in the city and miraculously find you £5 million (less than this and they are probably not interested). What you are not aware of at the time is that you've just sold your soul and your business and everything that was worthwhile about being your own boss. Anyway this is not a 'How to start a business with a whopping £5 million quid' book. This is about how to start a business for a more reasonable sum which won't involve you swapping a life with one or two bosses for five frantic years trying to please ten egomaniacs with time and money on their hands. Two-thirds of all venture capital start-ups in the US are sold within three years. Hardly long-term meaningful endeavours.

Grants

This is more like it – free money. And it often really is. Despite all the cynicism surrounding the Department for Business, Innovation and Skills (formerly the Department for Trade and Industry, and likely to be called something else in the future) and the EU and new government initiatives, there are some very good ones out there, set up with worthy intentions and fulfilling real needs of real people. The only major pitfalls are:

- It is very difficult to get any proper information about everything that is available. Local enterprise agencies will give you some information, the internet will get you some snippets; but ultimately, and this goes for EU grants too, all roads lead to the DBIS and garnering facts is often about as easy as translating ancient Hebrew using a Dutch phrase book. Not impossible, just difficult and frustrating – so be prepared to persevere.

- The individual awards often do not allow you to receive any other kind of government grant for a number of years, so pick one with care.

- You almost always need some of your own money or a bank's as well, and the grant or award is not for start-ups but for businesses that have been trading profitably for some time.

The types of government and EU money available are, broadly, the following:

Competition

Description: Awards based on a competition with other rival companies going for the same money.

Strengths: The amounts are often quite high (around £50,000-£150,000) and the competitions are generally under-subscribed. Often they are for technological innovation, so this is good if you plan to manufacture anything from software to a new type of waterbed.

Pitfalls: You either need a track record (usually you should have been trading for around five years) or about one-third of the total amount of the money you need should come from your own resources. So, not for us.

Enterprise finance guarantee (EFG)

Description: Replaces the loan guarantee scheme but basically seems pretty much the same thing. The money actually comes from your local bank in the form of a loan, most of which is guaranteed by the DBIS (around 90%), payable over roughly ten years at a reasonable rate of interest.

Strengths: With this you don't have to put your house on the line, so the risk is very low. Again, the amount can be quite high at around £50K.

Pitfalls: Firstly, banks really do not want to get involved in this little government initiative, when they can loan money to you without all that DBIS red tape and a load of bureaucrats peeking over their shoulder. The government also puts a premium on the loan (about 2%), which makes for fairly expensive borrowing. Again, they usually won't even consider you until you have been trading for some time and the award is mutually exclusive. This means you cannot get a £50K loan guarantee and then go for an EU award as described above for the other two thirds. I know, I've tried. Again, not for us, I fear.

Government benefits

Description: Basically unemployment benefit, payable for a period of three months whilst you 'test' your business idea.

Strengths: Fairly easy to get if you have a glimmer of a good business plan. There are not many strings attached. Like most things that seem to work in life it's a curious mix of the cynical and idealistic. On the one hand it is just a good way to get people off the unemployment register and on the other it could be the motivation needed for those people who have entrepreneurial flair but are unable to get a job that reflects their abilities. You get to talk to plenty of business advisors along the way about anything from accounting to marketing, and you get to meet loads of people in a similar position to you, who you can try your ideas out on.

Having something like this in place could also help when getting a bank loan, as they can see you have some income.

Pitfalls: Let's face it, it's not a lot of money and some of the meetings you go to can drag horribly and make you wish you still were standing in the dole queue. That being said, with the award you can also get part of your mortgage or rent paid by the housing benefit office and receive tax credits if you have children. Add all this together and, depending on your personal circumstances, you could be looking at £100-£150 a week for the first few months, plus free dental and eye care. It's not bad for a few afternoons' work, and some of the advisors really know their stuff.

It takes the raw edge off the difficult period at the start and you can combine it with other forms of loan. It works well for people without much in the way of savings. It can also be combined with tax credits.

A note on awards

The Prince's Trust Award is slightly different in that it is for people between 18 and 30. There is a grant for people who are genuinely disadvantaged (about £4000 at the time of writing) and an award of about £1500. If you fit the criteria it is an excellent way to start out.

If you do not fit the award criteria, Business Link may be able to point you in the direction of a business angel. These can be anyone from all walks of life but crucially they have money and time enough on their hands to pitch in with start-up funds and good advice. It is rarely more than £100K and they tend to be more kindly than a venture capitalist.

Loans

Small bank loan

Description: Most high street banks will lend you between £3K and £5K, without guarantees, paid off over a five-year period (at around £200 a month).

Strengths: Easy loan to get, you really don't even need to spend too much time seeing people at the bank; one or two short visits and a reasonably good business plan is all you need. Good to get in conjunction with the EFG (enterprise finance guarantee) funding and quite sufficient for starters. If the business is doing well after another year you can increase the amount, in the form of another slightly bigger loan or an overdraft facility.

Pitfalls: Loans come with interest repayments and these have to be considered. With the ridiculously low rates at the moment the cost of a business loan over five years of £5K would be somewhere in the region of £800. You may also need to show you have put some of your own money into the venture (around £1000 minimum).

Still, it's not a lot of money and the bank will probably leave you alone to get on with things. No one is going to take away your house or your car if you don't pay it back, either.

Family loan

Description: Maiden Aunts, doting godparents, accommodating (or perhaps just resigned) mother and father. Most of us are lucky enough to have at least one of these.

Strengths: Blood is, after all, thicker than water.

Pitfalls: Everyone's family is different; the family connection could become an added stress or a pillar of strength. Only you know. London Tutors, my first business, really started in 1991 with a £1000 gift from my late grandfather. In the last ten years, I have variously worked with my mother (two years!), my father, and my eldest brother. It has its moments but it works for me.

Some brief notes on approaching investors

With friends and family, enquire of them first if they want to be approached. Do not outline to someone your ideas and ask them to give you some money all in the same conversation.

In the case of institutions, like banks, find out what their procedures are for considering applications and go along with it. Have your business plan ready but be prepared to restyle it to suit their criteria. It's a bit time-consuming but part of the game.

With both, stick like glue to the 30-second rule. If it doesn't sound good to start with, then you'll not get past first base.

Things to Watch Out For

Congenital laziness

Actually this is not strictly true. Some of the biggest achievers in history have been real slobs. Benjamin Franklin was apparently lazy but very driven – not only was he a successful politician, he also found the time to invent the lightning rod, glass armonica, Franklin stove, bifocal glasses and the flexible urinary catheter. Franklin never patented his inventions, possibly because he never got around to it.

Also it is a perfectly worthy thing to go into business for yourself if you are lazy. It is no sin to waste your own time, just other people's[*]. *The most important thing is how effective you are when you do actually do some work.* Some people are amazingly efficient or bright and

---

[*] Laziness also shouldn't be confused with uninterest. An example of complete dispassion that very possibly led to his downfall is Louis XVI who, on the day the Bastille was stormed, wrote in his diary, 'Nothing happened'.

really only need to work a couple of hours a day to make a decent living. But, of course, only some people. For others, that's a siren call to disaster.

The real problem for everyone is action. Wanting to do something is very different from bringing an idea to fruition. Most businesses fail to get properly off the ground because in their heart of hearts the key person cannot actually see it becoming a success and, in consequence, they lack follow-through. If you cannot clearly visualise how something is to become a success and be at least 80% sure that you are the one to pull it off in one way or another, then put this book down and have a long heart to heart with yourself about your prospects. You've got to be motivated.

Money

I will qualify this by saying that, in my experience, I have never seen someone make a success of a business if they use it merely as a vehicle for earning. Lasting, meaningful businesses are built by people who:

- care about what they do

- care about what other people think of the business.

Call it their reputation, or customer service, if you will, but it really seems to be true what the management consultants say. People don't buy from a business, they buy from people. They would rather purchase from a business with a human side; call it a personality – the marketing gurus call it 'identity'.

A study carried out by James C. Collins and Jerry Porras called *Built to Last: Successful Habits of Visionary Companies* looked at a series of well-known companies that have endured for numerous decades (some from the 1890s) to the present day. Nearly all the really successful ones started life with a clear and definite ideology to create a lasting entity and not a primary goal to make money.

Disney is the perfect example. It is less a corporation and more an idea, says Mr J. Fowler in his excellent book, *Prince of the Magic Kingdom*. He says, and I quote:

> *This is not a corporate history. It is a history of a deeply human struggle over ideas, values, and hopes…values at times so evanescent that some people could dismiss them as silly, values so deep that other dedicated their careers to making them come alive.*

It's a perfectly reasonable proposition when you think about it. You would hardly warm to an individual whose character was such that you could not identify with them – or was such that you felt they were incompetent, greedy or dishonest. And even so, your business should display a very clear and wholesome personality. Suffusing a business with agreeable qualities takes time, and above all requires that someone, ultimately you, cares enough about it to imbue into it some of the more amiable aspects of their own character.

However, some very clever people have said in the past that being good at what you do is all that counts and that riches will follow, regardless. Granted, this is sometimes the case. Nevertheless, I know plenty of people who are very talented and good at what they do and who are vastly under-appreciated and underpaid.

If you just want to make money, invest in shares in a bear market or buy property anywhere in the south east after about 2011. If you want to create something meaningful, think about why the company you are trying to build is important to you, what characteristics you would like it to have and then concentrate on building this into a business identity.

Ideas, or complete lack thereof

You have to have a good idea. This may seem obvious to you and me but you would be amazed how many would-be business-founders give up their jobs, remortgage their house, buy a laptop and convert the spare room into a make-shift place of work, only to sit down on Day One and realise that the idea they had wasn't a very good one. It sounds extreme but this has happened to people I know.

An idea does not need to be earth-shatteringly innovative to be good. In fact, inventive ideas generally take a long time to get off the ground. A solid business idea, which you know to have worked for others, is quite often the best. You just need to decide why it will work for you.

For example: we all know coffee shops work because we pass them virtually everyday and they can't all be trading in debt. But will your coffee shop work and why?

Likewise, you do not need to be a creative thinker to start a business. This is one of the great fallacies of entrepreneurship. I dislike and distrust those self-help books that tell you what type of person you need to become to be a successful person. This is not just because of how smug they tend to sound but also because the notion that all successful people come from the same basic mould is clearly not true.

If I was pressed on the subject and really had to give an answer, I would say the attribute I valued most in an entrepreneur was Common Sense. Problems never go away in business and the ability to deal with them is 50% experience and 50% common sense.

Useful Websites

www.businesslink.gov.uk

Helped me with everything from how to do basic accounts, sales, marketing and a business plan.

www.direct.gov.uk

Advice on everything from how much tax to pay, to your rights as a self-employed person.

www.companieshouse.gov.uk

Company registration, checking whether company names have already been nabbed, looking at competitors' accounts.

www.hmrc.gov.uk

Useful pages on tax (again).

www.bbc.co.uk/business

Auntie is reassuringly helpful, with info on setting up, money management and so on.

2.

Making Money

In which we start making money.

Basic Strategies

- Having a perfect grasp of your cash flow for at least the next 12 months is essential. Check your bank statement, your income and your expenses at least once every three days. Never let anything become a nasty surprise.

- The simplest and possibly most effective start-up strategy is to keep the overheads lower than your immediate competition and you'll be able to win business purely by undercutting them.

- Keep the business flexible in terms of structure and what it sells or what services it offers (within reason, of course).

- Always have a back-up plan for when you aren't making much money at the start, i.e. a second job or income stream you can fall back on at short notice.

- Never enter into a negotiation on price without knowing the market value of what you are discussing and what you are prepared to pay. Even avoid asking for a quotation if you don't know roughly what you should expect to be paying.

- Plan the coming week's goals and tick them off as you achieve them. It sounds childish but it can be strangely satisfying. For the first few months of a business you will be constantly walking around remembering things that you should be doing. It will give you a small sense of achievement to prioritise these things and strike them through when they are accomplished and, believe me, at the start you'll take your achievements in any form.

- Commit numbers and names and meetings to memory, otherwise you'll constantly have your head in a diary or a notebook and you won't get any real work done. If this is too hard, get into the habit of logging everything – maybe get an iPhone or PDA for this.

- Learn how to switch off. Don't be afraid to take time off at unusual moments. My particular favourite was afternoon films at the cinema. It will make you remember why you are doing this in the first place. Becoming so focused that you lose track of the fun in running your own show is more often the real reason why people give up after a year or so.

- If you are working from the spare room, chances are, you'll only need the use of an impressive place to meet once in a while. Local job centres and even libraries often have cheap or indeed free meeting rooms available. If not, a good restaurant is the perfect alternative for small meetings.

The necessity of momentum

A friend of mine started a successful catering business in Yorkshire with less than two months' working capital. If it had not started taking money in eight weeks, then he would have been back to his old job with Halifax Council, at his old desk, quietly hoping that no one had noticed he'd ever left. He'd worked for caterers in the past and knew that they relied heavily on local Yellow Pages advertising. Sadly, this was pre-Yell.com and the printed version of the Yellow Pages only came out once a year and took weeks to hit people's doorsteps, so this was not an option. Necessity being the mother of invention, he got on the phone instead and rang everyone he could think of, not stopping until he had five meetings with local events organisers. He then turned up at each meeting with a contract bearing his signature and the promise of a 20% discount for an advance booking.

He never looked back – but he did say in hindsight that he would never have been so bullish were it not for the fact that he couldn't face going back to his old life.

Whatever it takes, you must keep the momentum going now or things can just tail off for a few months and before you know it you won't be all that interested in the business anymore.

Planning black holes

Just as some of us hate to plan, others love it – perhaps a little too much. Most of us have wasted hours formulating lists or revision timetables for tasks we really don't want to do; it's a perfectly human way of keeping the inevitable at bay.

In this case, having spent so much physical and emotional energy setting the business up, the prospect of it failing before it has really got off the ground is too much to bear for some. 'Still putting things in place' is a simple enough excuse and one you hear a lot. But once the seed capital is there it must be put to use immediately, especially if it is a loan, as this money is costing you more money every day in interest. Also, it is dithering and indecisiveness at this stage that, nine times out of ten, makes a business fail, as opposed to the idea being a bad one. Keep this in mind: if your idea was that bad you would most probably not have got the money in the first place.

Marketing

Not to be dismissive, because many people's livelihood is based on imparting to other people, at great expense, the principles of marketing with a capital M. However it is my belief that all such Marketing, in its purest form, is a success only unto itself.

By this I mean that it is a theoretical and fascinating subject, whose greatest gift is the payment of fees to the legions of consultants who preach it in all its forms. The good that it will do you at this stage is negligible, if you try and put the theory into practice.

However there are certain aspects of what is known as the 'marketing mix' which will be important. These include:

Brand image

The personality of the business that you are running – its 'brand image', some might say. Is it up-market and discerning or is it more approachable than that? Are you aiming for the budget end of the market? This will affect everything from the type of logo you opt for, to the stationary you buy and the website you build. Even what you wear to work. It's not impossible, but it is extremely unlikely that the brand image you create will be all-encompassing, i.e.

quality/budget/friendly/discerning. Your personality will help you decide this as much as anything.

Publicity

Once you know what kind of an image you want to portray, how do you set about getting that across? Sometimes it is a fairly passive process. You design a logo, website and brochure around a concept and you let people make up their own minds about you. This isn't necessarily a bad thing. You may have decided to be a bit more flexible in the early days. This is fine, as long as you do keep in mind that you have to develop a clear identity sooner or later otherwise you will not be making the most of your company. You may want to be more pro-active, so write press releases, leaflets, take out ads, etc. Again this isn't a bad thing, especially if yours is the sort of business that is very fresh and original and you want to make a name for yourself early on. However, as ever, keep in mind the costs. There's plenty of free publicity to be had out there, and the press, local or otherwise, are always keen on a story as long as it is original and very human.

Targeting

So you've got your image, you have a reasonable idea how to put this across – but you won't be able to do anything until you make up your mind as to *who* you want to target. This would have been handled fairly extensively in the business plan; now you have to make it a reality.

One key thing I have learnt is that it is better to get a clear message across to a few people, than a general message to a very varied audience. An example of this is press releases: for years I toiled away writing articles and press releases for the dailies and weeklies of this great nation, with little or no success. Not to say we did not get any press coverage – I had a weekly column in a national business magazine for a bit, a long *Guardian* article once about translation, and a few spots on BBC4 and BBC2. But nothing meaningful ever came of it. No one ever became a client because they heard me on *Woman's Hour* talking about home tuition. However, about three years ago I wrote a press release to our local paper about languages, which was turned into a quarter-page interview in the middle of the paper. And the response was instant: several local businesses were moved to contact us the following week and gave us their business. Despite so-called globalisation, local market appeal can be a very strong marketing tool.

Sales

This is an art form. If you cannot learn to sell it's going to be very tough for you indeed. Selling has a bad reputation because so many people who are in sales are so hopeless or sleazy.

It is a fact of life that the best sales people will not even let you become aware you've just been sold something. Instead you'll go away with the warm feeling that you have just made a brilliant decision to buy something and what's more you probably really like the person you bought it from.

Personally I've sold aerial pictures door to door, I've flogged insurance, handed out helium balloons dressed as a clown (sometimes as a cowboy). I've sold advertising space in magazines, sandwiches direct to undergraduates in their rooms (my first real business). I've sold books to shops, alcohol to pubs, not to mention all the various services my companies offer. Some of this is hard sell, some of it is a slower, softly, softly process.

The main thing to remember is that people generally only buy something they don't actually have a pressing need for if they like you. Unless they are desperate, they're not going to like you if they imagine that you are only interested in their money. They are not going to buy from you if you make them feel stupid, if you bully them, if you suck-up too much and if you don't connect with them on some very human level.

So be yourself and learn how to talk to people on a natural person-to-person basis. This is the key.

Find the niche

If you are selling anything, your first job is to identify the niche markets in your industry and undercut the competition by around 10-20%. This is easier than it sounds, as larger businesses are nearly always trying to cover a far greater area in terms of what they do and where they do it than is strictly in their best interests. Simply stated, this means that much of their activity is actually a drain on their resources and consequently is putting their overheads up. Your primary concern is to identify the profitable areas (if you know your business and you've done your research, this shouldn't be hard), establish a low-cost concern and beat them at their own game.

It's a numbers game

Selling is also nearly always a numbers game. Simply put, the more people you approach, the greater the chance you have of success. When we started out approaching people to see if they would buy translations from us, on the first half-dozen calls I managed to win the contract to translate the marketing for the video launch of the film *Jurassic Park* (a £22K contract) and translation work for a central London hospital who still use us regularly today. This was just beginner's luck, because for the next year we didn't really manage to sell anything. I was beginning to doubt that our method was right. In actual fact it was, but doing only an hour's selling a day wasn't enough. It took me two hard years to work this out. I duly increased it to three hours a day and took on someone to do one day a week as well; we saw our turnover triple in a year.

For me, then, the secret to my first success in business was finding out exactly what amount of sales effort was effective. To be frank, two years to find that out was too long.

After sixteen years this is fairly refined and I can usually predict on a good year/bad year basis the number of days selling required to produce what number of leads which in turn will give us x increase in turnover within a certain period.

It may take you a few years to get the equation more or less right but the formula is indispensable if you don't want to lie awake at night wondering if you've done enough.

The trick with any sales pitch is finding out, seemingly as innocently as possible, what the client might want from you, and steering the conversation in such a way that lets them reach the conclusion that you are the person who can supply it.

It can be broken down into the following elements:

Introduction

Saying hello and who you are.

Definition

Ascertaining what they want, if anything, out of the range of things you are selling. Usually just a few straight questions will sort this out.

Pitch

Tell them what you have to offer.

Answer objections

Tell them why you're the best person who can supply it.

Price build-up

Illustrate why you are good for business on a purely commercial level.

Close

Basically, are they going to buy what you are selling?

***

Depending on your chosen field, some of the elements may not be strictly relevant but this about sums it up.

The hard sell

Hard sell is when you approach someone, face to face or on the phone, as one perfect stranger to another and you take them through all the above stages before the encounter is over. It is probably the hardest form of selling because all the elements have to be gone through before the person either walks off or punches you for annoying them. When I sold door-to-door we never did call backs, as experience showed them to be a waste of time for that kind of sale. All elements of the process, including the close, were done and dusted in one 20-minute visit. It was hard because you had to warm the client up in no more than a minute or so and, once you had their attention, you had no more than three to five minutes to close the deal. The trick was to turn it into an impulse buy. With no fixed salary (we got about £10 commission per sale) it was knackering, but good training.

The soft sell

Not all businesses need to do a hard sell, nor is it often even appropriate. There is a type of salesperson who believes that the only time you are really working is when yelling down the phone at someone. Soft sell is the alternative and it is up to you to decide when to use which method. It is important to keep in mind that soft sell is exactly the same as the hard sell but operates over a longer period of time, sometimes months or even years. You are doing the same thing, so the steps you take to get the client from the introduction to the close are identical.

Success

One final thing to remember is that it is a myth that some people like selling and others don't. Nobody likes to hear the word 'No' several times a day and even the most thick-skinned are likely to start taking it personally after a bit.

However, when done right, the rewards are spectacular. There is, quite simply, nothing like the feeling of going out and winning business for yourself. Like many things that take a certain degree of bravado at the outset, once you are over the first hurdle, you will forget the rejections and remember only the successes. You get a feeling approaching euphoria when you make a difficult sale (I'm only half exaggerating here) and it actually becomes quite addictive.

Stay flexible

As with cash flow, in sales you should aim to keep flexibility at all costs. Just as you should not commit your money to one course without having substantial reserves, nor should you commit the company to one rigid marketing goal. Do enough to see if something will work but be prepared to modify approach and investment if something isn't working. Keeping this system in mind will also maintain your creativity and allow for a constant 'tinkering' with the marketing mix.

For example, about a year ago I noticed that our local framer seemed to have an eye for reasonably priced local artists as opposed to plastering the walls with reproduction pictures of ballerinas or kittens with bow ties. Over a period of a few months his shop evolved into a Mecca for affordable art (although this is the Home Counties we're talking about). I'm sure the picture framing business does fairly well as it's been there years, but the subtle change in direction has not only vastly increased traffic into his shop but also helped a lot of unknown artists in the area get noticed.

As an entrepreneur you should almost constantly be doubting your decisions (though not your abilities) and reflecting on whether you are doing your best whatever the state of the business. Testing your decisions, once taken, should become second nature.

It's an unarguable fact that people make money all the time in all sorts of places in all sorts of businesses and in good and bad markets. You can too, if you learn to adapt before you are forced to.

Price Negotiation

Sooner or later you are going to have to have a conversation with somebody that starts with the words, 'Can we have a word about this quote...?' Either it is going to be you saying this to a potential supplier or a client ringing you up to get some money knocked off the bill. Generally there are two incorrect responses to both – namely a) 'Certainly, how much were you thinking?' and b) 'Bugger off'. Neither is especially helpful, as the latter merely invites more swearing and lost business and the former opens the door to any one of several ridiculous suggestions that will cost you money.

At the outset of this section, it is also worth noting that any sort of bartering or haggling implies a certain lack of trust. To move away from this regrettable but wholly understandable state of affairs, it is important to concentrate at the start on making any discussion about money into a sort of partnership where both parties are trying to attain a common goal (a mutually beneficial business arrangement mostly). This infers that you are problem-solving together, not having a fight.

If at all possible, it is best to have a negotiation over two or more conversations. Initially all that is required is for you to listen to the second party's point of view. It is vitally important that you then crave some thinking time. Even if it is just five minutes and you call them back, it prevents any quick-fire horse-trading, where you almost inevitably end up meeting in the middle; and, more importantly, it is invaluable as a technique for preventing things getting heated. When people get upset they tend to get dogged and this helps no one.

Some compromise is almost inevitable, unless you are very sure of yourself. Most importantly, if you are to give any ground or they are to do the same, it must be for a clearly defined reason. Put the phone down after politely letting them know that you will be getting back to them shortly. Then marshal your arguments and phone them back. Try and avoid emailing at this stage – there is something about this form of communication that has an uncanny knack of allowing a minor difference of opinion to escalate into a franker exchange of views than is strictly necessary.

Essentially what you are aiming for is consensus on why something should cost what is being charged. If you are negotiating your costs with a client, this should be something you have already thought about in depth. One of the central issues in any pricing policy you set out is justification for your charges based on the accepted market rate. If there isn't a 'going price' then work out the cost to you, plus your time getting an end product or service to them. No one expects someone to lose money but, as a rule of thumb, anything over a 100% margin on your physical costs might be considered excessive. If margins are not relevant to your business or are complex to work out on a job-by-job basis, then work out a rough hourly rate that covers all your costs plus around 20%. By the same token you should expect the same sort of logic from suppliers.

Honesty really is the key word. Honest. People will pick up on a line or a ruse very quickly and whilst they might be polite enough not to say anything it will sour the relationship. You might not mind if this is a supplier (although you should) but you can do a lot of damage in just a few minutes to a client relationship that has taken months to build.

Whilst I'm about it, here are a few techniques that might be employed by those clients wishing to get a better deal:

Hilarity

The most obvious ruse and one which wouldn't even fool my four-year-old son. Eyes wide, the negotiator treats anything you say with an incredulous, 'You've got to be kidding!' An extreme form of this is when he or she falls over in mock surprise, clutching at his chest, as if in the throws of a seizure.

Step over the prone body on the way out the door and talk later.

Grim silence

A good one this. The other person simply says nothing, whilst fixing you with a steely gaze they've practised in the bathroom mirror. The hope here is that you'll be embarrassed or intimidated into filling the silence with more concessions. Concentrate on settling your features into a serene expression. I find that mentally humming the theme tune to *Neighbours* helps. The contented, faraway look in your eye will eventually unnerve the other person and you can then start to get your own back.

An alternative to silence is when the negotiator adopts a stammer, tempting you to finish his sentences for him, usually in his favour. Again, this should be met with a Zen-like calm and a silent insistence that they furnish their own arguments.

Dishonesty

By that I mean the person you are talking to adopts a devious response to any suggestion you make with, 'I thought you said...' and then usually tells you something they'd like you to have said but that has no basis in reality. The idea is to break your flow by putting you firmly on the defensive, and, you never know, you might find yourself admitting to something that never happened. Like silence, the only way out of this is to fight fire with fire. Disagree with a sad shake of the head and adopt a similarly hurt tone at being so misunderstood. Then leave it there. Do not be tempted to try and put words into their mouth, unless you have decided that negotiations are past saving.

Volume or loss leader

The client promises much more work or better rates of pay 'next time'. Use your own judgement here about volumes, but in my experience loss leaders very rarely play out well for the vendor. Once you have agreed on a deal, particularly one that is very favourable to the other party, then they are very unlikely to want to revise it.

Decision maker

Just when you think you've got them beat they turn around and say, 'I agree with what you are saying but my boss will never go for it'. Permit yourself a thin smile and then ask to speak to 'the decision maker'.

Wrong conclusions

Never let someone you don't fully trust sum things up before you have a chance to. This is because they are very likely to say, 'Let me sum up...' and then they proceed to give everything a favourable spin in their direction. If they do get in first, make every effort to give the impression you're just not listening: open a packet of crisps, yawn halfway through one of their key sentences and turn your head away to stare out of the window at something happening in the middle distance.

When they've quite finished, say nothing for a few moments and then remark (still staring out the window) that you've just seen a cloud that looks like a cat. This is incredibly annoying for the other person. Whilst they are fighting off the urge to stab you in the eyeball with their pen you then regain the advantage, if not the moral high ground, by summing up their summary – being careful to bring the facts back into play.

Establishing a Routine

Let's face it, there are plenty of small business out there but the vast majority of us work for other people. It is very likely, then, that you are going to be feeling a couple of country miles shy of your comfort zone at the outset of running your own business. One of the best ways to get over this is to establish a daily routine alongside a firm set of principles, which will be the cornerstone of your company ethic.

First of all, get used to looking at your business with a critical eye and deciding if things are working or not. If all is well then great, if not, have a back-up plan that is quick and easy to implement.

I'll coin a phrase now and call it the **Principle of Prudence**. The worst-case scenario, in any business, is that after paying expenses, electricity, the telephone bill, etc., you don't have any money left to pay yourself. A lot of people throw the towel in at this stage and go back to working in a shop/office/etc. However, I have found myself in this position before and most of you will too. The main thing is not to panic and imagine that you've failed.

Before starting a business, **make sure that you have a source of income that is relatively accessible** at short notice to tide you over in the difficult periods. There is no shame in this and it doesn't mean that your business is rubbish. Remind yourself that if you started out with £100K, then you wouldn't need to do this but then you'd have this enormous debt hanging over you too. I used to teach French and English privately. Earning £20 an hour, I only needed to do three to four hours a day to keep body and soul together and still have time to run and grow the business. It is a source of comfort now to know that I can go back to this and earn £20K a year without too much trouble and without giving up on the long-term goal.

Starting things on **a tight budget focuses the mind** and you become very aware of making lazy decisions. I do believe that big budget start-ups kick-off in a spendthrift manner, which colours the way they operate in the future. With the smallness of the budget you must learn never to solve a problem by chucking money at it. Never take a quote at face value or assume that just because everybody engages a bookkeeper, web designer or has an expensive brochure that there is not another cost-free way. There are literally thousands of ways to cut costs and still get the same service, or achieve what you want. The key is ingenuity. Lazy rich people, when defending themselves, always claim that they need the money to allow them to focus on the job of running the business without bothering about the small stuff. This is poppycock, God is in the details and it's in mastering the small stuff that you learn how to run the big stuff with clarity, innovation and rigour. As the owner, you are never above the details. As soon as you leave this to someone else, costs will spiral; just see if they don't.

By way of example, we never buy advertising on spec. Untried advertising in anything – magazines, the Yellow Pages, internet banners – represents an unacceptable risk in my view. Giving someone £1000 to put an ad in their publication with no guarantees has always struck me as reckless and stupid. We do advertise, it is an important way of getting work; but we insist on getting the first advert for free. If we get some response, then we will spend money because we know that this is a good investment. Magazines, in particular, always have a bit of space free at the end of the month, a quarter page near the back, or maybe a few column centimetres to fill in the classifieds. Persuading them to give you a small bit for free, on the understanding that they will be creating a loyal customer if it works, is relatively easy and no one loses out.

Some cost-cutting, however, is just penny pinching and counterproductive. We never had proper letter heading for the first three years of being in business and in hindsight this was a mistake that probably cost us a lot of clients. Spend money on image. This includes making sure you have enough phone lines so that it doesn't ring engaged.

Keep your **personal expenses to a minimum**. It's not impossible but it's not a great idea either to start a small business if you've got a £3000 monthly mortgage and four children in private school. Do everything you can to take the pressure off yourself and to keep the business in the black. Take in lodgers if need be. Most people generally cut costs when things have got bad. You have to learn to be more pre-emptive and have costs down long before money becomes a problem.

With regard to flexibility, always have an eye for creating a structure that can **grow and diminish at minimal cost to you** in a relatively short space of time, should disaster strike. Having freelance staff is one way, or two part-timers instead of one full-time assistant. This means that you can dispense of one part-timer's service in quiet periods and still have someone to help out, assuming there is some work to do.

Unfortunately, you have to learn to be ruthless in this. Keeping part-timers on temporary contracts allows for this and means that you are not letting anyone down by promising a career you have no certainty of offering them.

If you take on office space that becomes too much, then make sure you are able to sub-let at short notice. I know people who do this so successfully their office eventually ends up costing them nothing.

Go for leasing deals – although office machinery, including brand new computers, is so cheap these days as to make them a disposable commodity anyway. But you can lease coffee-making machines, franking machines and even office furniture (and what's more its 100% tax deductible).

Premises

Improved communications, mobile phones, email and a host of other Heath Robinson contraptions (if your office is anything like mine), mean that working from home is no longer merely a pleasant dream, particularly if you are running a services company.

It has an illustrious pedigree as well. Hewlett-Packard was started from someone's garden shed (possibly Hewlett's), as was Dell Computers and our very own Tesco, way back in 1919. More recently Peter Jones – of *Dragons' Den* fame – started his second venture working in an office which was also his bedroom, having lost all his money the first time round. Friends Reunited and Wikipedia were still run from the spare room long after they became worldwide brands. My personal favourite though is Charles Babbage, the English mathematician, philosopher, inventor and mechanical engineer who originated the concept of a programmable computer in his kitchen, effectively making the parlour at 44 Crosby Row, Walworth Road, London the real birthplace of Silicone Valley.

According to www.powerhomebiz.com, favourite working-from-home businesses these days include IT (who'd have guessed it?), childcare, antiques, sewing, import/export and, bizarrely, witchcraft.

Attitudes are changing as well; working from home is no longer looked down upon as the arena of the semi-retired accountant or a mother with time on her hands. Plenty of people work from home in all sorts of business. It suits the type of consultant who finds themselves in other peoples' offices for half the week, barristers who don't go to court much and even IT engineers who can fix things online with a powerful PC and a broadband connection.

It is not, however, for someone with a company, a brand name and who wants to give the impression of being more than just one man and his fax. I honestly don't know why but people don't like buying from a company they think is struggling or merely diminutive – the old adage that to be successful you need to seem successful is depressingly true in this context.

The following are some tips on how to keep these costs down:

- Find someone to **share an office** with. This can be ideal if you are both running similar size, complementary concerns and could even be a good source of new business. I share an office with a recruitment consultancy and we have both used each other's services (him translation, me sourcing staff) over the years. It also means I have someone to flick elastic bands at who cannot take me to an industrial tribunal and it's also nice to go for beer with a non-employee after work. The fact you are sharing often means you can afford slightly more space than if you were on your own – a meeting room that doesn't double as the stationery cupboard, for example, or a decent-sized kitchen.

- My first office was a **sub-let** in the head office of a very large firm who did not need all their space, so you might want to ask around with this in mind. For £100 a month I got to sit in brightly lit, well-furnished and warm surroundings. So very different from the dank, freezing environment that was the rotting barge I lived on at the time in Chelsea. I could also make free with their biscuits and photocopier.

- A few years back we **took over the last two years of a 15-year lease** in the centre of Henley-on-Thames. As the prices were effectively 15 years old, we managed to get two years' very cheap rent in a fabulous late-medieval building near the river, which we have now bought. One word of warning, though – when you have a lease re-assigned to you, check that the outgoing party makes good any repairs etc, otherwise you could well get hit for a new roof and a boiler a couple of years later.

- A former colleague of mine set up a management accounting firm in an almost absurdly cheap office in southwest London. I went to pick him up one evening on my way to the nearest pub. The offices themselves were tiny, more like a series of box rooms, each with a school desk, fan heater and grubby walls and were actually owned and rented out by the council who hadn't got around to reviewing the rents since around 1973. As it happened, the office shared a door and stairwell with the upstairs rooms of the local library. Directly opposite the accountant's door was a council library meeting room with all the old Edwardian furnishings. Over our first pint he explained to me that for about a fiver a morning he was able to greet clients at a large oak table surrounded by leather-bound volumes with a nice view of the park. People nearly always assumed that this fabulous room was actually part of his offices and that he must be a very respectable and successful accountant. He is now.

Nevertheless, this doesn't sort out the problem of who is going to be there to answer the phone when you're not there. No one is going to be wildly enthusiastic about your company if all they get is an answerphone message, nor is it an especially good idea to redirect calls to your mobile. Windy conversations beside busy roads might be okay for emergencies and conversations with friends but for first impressions they really don't sound good. And the key to starting out is worrying constantly about first impressions and creating an aura of success so people you want to be close to feel the same way too. Particularly clients.

Happily, if you really cannot afford an office and a receptionist there is a way around it at a cost of £50 a month.

Answering services

Pick one that is somewhere like Newcastle or Glasgow. Central London answering services are very expensive (often charging on volume of calls) and they are often too busy or large to care. Having someone answer your phone after ten to 15 rings and slightly mispronounce the name of your company in a listless tone of voice is less than good for your all-important image, so choose the company with care, and with an ear for first impressions.

The best answering services are small offices with one or two people who will answer the phone in a cheerful manner and those that will willingly undertake to ask the right questions and even give out basic information on your behalf. This gives the impression that the receptionist is part of the organisation and can be relied on to pass information to you, which is important. If clients instinctively feel that they have to speak to you for everything including the smallest and most frivolous trifle, then the chances are you'll have a nervous breakdown inside of two years.

In fact, I like this system so much that we still use a firm in the northeast, even though there are more than enough people now to answer the phone in the London office. BT provide a line that allows them to put through calls to us anywhere in the world, just like an expensive switchboard but without the costs of buying an expensive switchboard. It costs around £40 a quarter and it means that calls can be prioritised instead of taking up the time of people in the office who have been hired to do other things.

You are likely to change offices a fair bit in the first few years and phone dialling codes have a depressing habit of changing. To avoid spending a fortune on new letterheads and business cards each time you move, consider, if you will, the possibility of getting some specialist numbers that will stay with you forever.

A **freephone number** (at the time of going to press) costs you around 4p a minute, which isn't much, provided you learn to talk quickly. Clients do appreciate it and it gives the business an air of stability as well as a national feel, not a local trader impression.

If your business involves handing out information to people who stay on the phone for quite a while but rarely buy, then consider a **prefix number** that earns you money. It costs the caller between 6p and £1 a minute and you get a healthy percentage a minute back from the service provider, e.g. BT. This option can be very profitable too if you have the sort of business where masses of people phone.

Don't go for the expensive £1-plus-a- minute lines unless you really have got something valuable to say. People are wise to these now and they generally only work for sex lines and Saturday morning competitions for kids whose parents are still in bed.

An 0870 prefix used in conjunction with an 0800 free phone number works for us. The former for general enquiries, i.e. salespeople, and the latter for real clients who, as a rule, just love to get something for free.

Of course you need to already have a conventional line but your phone supplier will be able to 'point' the free phone number at this and the caller will ring seamlessly through to you.

Furthermore, if you really want to give a good impression, give someone the land line, saying something nonchalant like, 'This is my direct line'. This will make them feel important – just see if it doesn't.

The upshot, then, is that for the price of one conventional line rental and a paltry 4p a minute you give the impression of having three different lines at a stroke, one of which you actually make money off.

A note on fax lines

You might think you don't need one if you already have an internet connection (eFax is one such service; go online and read your faxes, just like email). This is fine but the quality is bad and it costs the client more money to send you a fax. If you do not feel up to an internet fax system, then do not, under any circumstances, have a shared phone and fax line.

Nothing sounds crappier for a company than having one of those messages that says, 'If you want to send Gerald Ltd a fax, please hold until the long beep and press the star key twice on your phone'. This is nearly always followed by what you judge to be a sort of a shortish beep that makes you hesitate and then you hear a clunking noise as you are disconnected.

Hiring for the First Time

You hopefully have started to make some money now and it's reasonable to assume you have built a positive cash flow. This is a happy position to be in. The problem, though, is that you are working a 13-hour day and still not getting everything done. So you look for help.

I suppose the main questions at this juncture are:

- What part of the business do I need help with?

- Can I afford it?

Office manager

Commonly we look for someone to answer the phones whilst we're out, do the filing, mail letters, that sort of thing. When I first started out my primary concern was to have a PA of my own I could ask to do various jobs I secretly thought were beneath me – return messages and, to my everlasting shame, collect my washing.

The problem is twofold. First of all, unless you can pay them a great deal no one wants to be anybody's PA for very long, especially if this is the sort of PA who is the at the bottom of the ladder because they're the only other employee in the company. I had three in one year and gave up. This is in direct contrast to PAs for important bosses who run large companies. They reside somewhere near the top of the hierarchy, just after the boss's spouse, but above everyone else. And they're often the only person who knows what is going on.

Secondly, there is not much need for a PA these days, as you already have a phone answering service, and you are probably perfectly capable of typing your own letters and popping them in the box on your way home.

Accountant

An accountant is expensive. I did a quick survey at the time of writing this, and came up with a typical figure of around £60 per hour.

When starting out, I decided that I would do my own accounts and that it would be a good learning curve. This stood me in very good stead for the first year and I learnt a lot, certainly quite enough to know what passes for an intelligent question for an accountant and what does not. The distinction is important; a fully qualified accountant is like any specialist, if they suspect they are dealing with someone who doesn't know the ropes, then they'll fleece you (legally, of course) at the first available opportunity. Knowledge is a very profitable commodity, if handled right.

Once you've learnt the basics, though, continue to do your accounts yourself but have them looked over by someone who is trained, before submitting them to HM Revenue & Customs. Learn from me, because in my third year I submitted my own accounts without having them looked over by a professional and it cost me money I could ill-afford at the time. The errors I made were the sort any accountant could have spotted.

This approach will only cost between £500 and £1000 per annum, depending on how complicated your (financial) affairs are. Most importantly, provided you choose someone good, it will save you at least that much in avoidance of unnecessary tax payments.

A bookkeeper is cheaper (around £15 per hour) but is really only useful if you are raising more than 50 invoices a month, paying around 100 suppliers in the same period and turning over something in excess of 300K per annum. And even then, you'll probably only need them once a week.

Anyway, after faffing about with PAs in various guises, I decided to keep admin my domain for a while longer and got some help with sales instead. As I have already mentioned, for us, this was the big turning point for the company. I had always maintained that you could only sell for yourself and that if it was your own company then you were your own best front. This is still the case but, as said, sales are nearly always as much a numbers game as one which relies on a quality-focused effort. By this I mean that a large database of potential clients turned out to be infinitely better than a small listing of surefire ones.

What was holding us back until then was that I was spending too much time courting potentially large clients I knew needed our services. It was working to an extent, in that we were growing – but we were growing very slowly. The new sales person's job was essentially contacting large numbers of not-so-large and not-so-surefire customers on a daily basis. In consequence we doubled turnover the following year and did the same again two years running.

The other benefit was that we were adding to our core clients lots of smaller clients, meaning we were less reliant on a few sources of income for our bread and butter. We also had a broad range of clients in many more industries to help us through harder times. Without realising it we had hit upon one of the most crucial aspects of running a successful service industry in that all industries are never in recession all at the same time. It follows, that if you are running a service industry try and service as many clients in different sectors and sizes as possible to avoid losing out when the market changes. Also, as became apparent during the 2007-2009 financial crisis, a large company is more likely to go under in certain circumstances than its small to medium-sized counterpart.

How do you know if you can afford it?

Before looking at full-time staff, you should be looking at having a positive cash flow for the next four months at least, after you have calculated your expenses and assumed that you might not make much money in the intervening period.

You can do this via a loan or you can do this with a sizeable overdraft facility. In my experience this is all very well but the best businesses are the ones that don't rely on handouts. It may take longer but provided your sales function is working and you have a reasonable source of income that is guaranteed, then what is the hurry?

Sometimes people take on staff when they are getting into difficulties in the belief that well-picked personnel will be able to turn the company around. This may well be the case but it is generally the exception in my experience and not the rule. I would say that more often it is the final nail in the coffin of a beleaguered company, so think long and hard before you go saddling yourself with any extra expenses when you are struggling.

Being in a hurry involves taking risks and forcing decisions about where the business is going before you are good and ready and often before you understand your own market enough to make those sort of vital decisions. As discussed earlier, at all times keep the risk element down to a minimum. This is the key to doing things on a shoestring and making a success of it. It will save you sleepless nights and your bank will appreciate it.

Freelance or PAYE?

Freelance costs you more and could land you in trouble if someone is coming to your office on a regular basis. This is with the possible exception of a bookkeeper or IT worker but make sure before paying anyone like this gross (without deducting the tax) that their local tax office is aware that they are self-employed and agrees with it. If not, you could end up footing their national insurance.

Taking staff on with contracts and deducting tax at source (PAYE, pay as you earn) worries people, usually for two reasons. The amount of paperwork needed with employees is daunting; contracts need to be drawn up and are expensive. The most cost-effective way is to borrow the wording from a contract of employment of a friend or family member. Check with a local solicitor if you are unsure, but it will cost money. As for deductions and tax implications, I once tried to do our payroll taking into consideration income tax, NI, etc. It's perfectly possible to do but time consuming if you don't know what you are doing and very boring, even with the appropriate software packages. Ask your new best friend (i.e. your accountant) if they will do it. The cost is usually around £15 pa per person and then all you need do once a month is issue cheques (or bank payments) according to the amounts on the payslips he or she provides.

Currently HMRC do an online PAYE calculation service. So far untried by me, but it sounds like a good idea.

Dismissing staff

A three-month trial period is legal and will allow you to see if you like them and if they are likely to become a valuable member of the team. If things go bad, then you can part company and it won't cost you a bean. If, after that, things go sour then you must provide the appropriate warnings (two verbal, one written and final) in the hope they will mend their ways. They may be holding out for a golden handshake and unfortunately some people have some strange notions about their entitlements; one year's salary after six months' employment has been quoted to me on occasion. They are, however, generally only entitled to two weeks' pay for the first couple of years of service and a few days extra for every year after that.

It's a nasty business asking people to leave and at times you will have to be crystal clear about the reasons why you are getting rid of them and what they can expect from you in terms of compensation. There is very little advice I can offer except make it quick, once you have decided to do it. There are obviously no euphemisms for telling someone they are no longer required. However, often they hate their job – just as anyone would dislike getting up early every morning to do something they are not terribly good at – and 'letting them go' is a relief for all concerned. Occasionally what you are doing will be met with disbelief and aggression, sometimes in the hope that this type of approach will get them more money. Work out what you are going to offer them beforehand, check that it fulfils the legal requirement as a minimum and do not waver from this.

A note on tax

If you have any questions about tax, then it's often simplest (and cheapest) to ask HMRC in person. They are helpful in general and, provided you insist on a written answer, will furnish you with the right answer. Contrary to popular belief, they are not there to rob you, rather to see that the law is carried out. Their advice, unlike an accountant's, is also free.

Useful Websites

www.businesslink.gov.uk

Sort of one-stop shop for small business advice and networking. Good place, generally, to start if you have a query or need advice from a real-life person.

www.employmentdocumentcompany.co.uk

Forms, packs, employers' guides, procedures and policy information. Everything here, document-wise, a business needs.

www.homeworking.com

If you must work from home, this is the best place for advice, case studies and miscellaneous information relating to running a business from the dining-room table.

www.propertyfinder.com

Commercial property has been in the doldrums the last couple of years but seems to be picking up. Some bargains about if you've made some money already.

www.businessballs.com

Way too much varied information in one place here and tricky to navigate, but some real gems (advice and anecdotal) if you are willing to trawl about.

3.

Growing Sensibly

In which we start to hammer out an infrastructure and craft a company culture.

Basic Strategies

- You simply cannot afford to be a Luddite. Keep as up-to-date with technology as possible.

- Invest in staff training. It costs much less than hiring experienced staff and if they are decent, they'll appreciate the cost and effort and repay you with hard work. Once trained you may lose a few people but actually fewer than you would think.

- Develop a company culture that is most in keeping with your personality – it takes much less effort to maintain this way.

- Staff should complement your talents, and not compliment you.

- To start with, don't think that you can just hire a load of other people to do the key tasks of sales, negotiation and cash flow management then go on an extended holiday. You must take this on yourself at first, then hand on responsibility in a controlled fashion.

Cash Flow

It's a bright morning mid-week in town. Clouds hang in the sky like individual puffs of cannon fire and people's contented faces are reflected in shop displays and the side windows of passing buses. As you saunter along the road, children gather in lively groups outside schools and you feel happy to be going to work.

One of the most enjoyable places to be in a business is the day you wake up to find that you have paid off what small debts you may have, cash flow is positive, salaries taken care of and you still have a bit over for growth.

For me the best bit about this was that I felt I could finally do things properly: new computers, a fax machine that didn't chew to shreds all it was given. Better letterhead, a cleaning lady who operated on the right side of the law and, the Holy Grail of any office, a proper tea and coffee-making machine as opposed to a sticky kettle, stuck in the corner sitting beside an empty biscuit tin.

One of the things that will get you to this point, apart from the selling, is good cash flow management. With any business, if money is going out faster than it is coming in, the business will fail sooner or later. Usually when the overdraft facility is stretched too far or, more likely, unexpectedly withdrawn. This is more common than one imagines. Simply because a high street bank is happy to lend you money on Tuesday, does not mean that by Friday they feel quite the same way. As far as they are concerned, it's their money (even if it isn't really) and they can ask for it back whenever they want. For this reason I have only ever had overdraft facilities as a security measure and have only called on them for a few days at a time in extremis (about six times in the last 12 years). This is perfectly possible if you abide by the following set of rules:

- Negotiate with suppliers where possible and where relevant arrange that you pay them only when you are paid. Make sure you are upfront about this. Suppliers will often agree to wait for payment if they are told of the situation in advance but will be understandably unimpressed if you spring this on them 30 days after they have invoiced. Using suppliers who are large companies is better, as they are less reliant on money coming in regularly.

- People often put any spare cash into a dividend payment or invest it into growing the business. Sometimes they'll even go back to the bank and use the increase in turnover to extend a borrowing facility, thereby putting themselves into greater debt. This is absolutely the wrong thing to do and sets off a company culture of debt, which will nearly always, sooner or later, end with the company going under. Debt is bad and eventually kills any company, bank or corporation. The first thing you need to do with any extra money is pay off any creditors. The second thing you do is build up a cash reserve equal to around six to 12 months' trading expenses for the business. Then pay yourself enough to do the same with your own personal accounts. It is only after you have done this that you may start to spend money on growth.

It is worth bearing in mind that once you have built up some cash reserves you can negotiate very good discounts with suppliers who you either pay upfront (somewhat risky, obviously) or on delivery of goods or services rendered.

Staff Relations

Control and management in two words. This doesn't of course mean that you turn into a despot overnight but it does mean that you're not going to get anywhere now without your staff's loyalty because it's in them, not you, that you now put the future of the company.

Make no mistake on this issue: at a certain point you are no longer actually running the business, you are managing other people to run it for you and there's a big difference.

There are plenty of books written by people who have looked into the subject more closely than I, but here are a few (very subjective) pointers.

- **Trust** people as much as you can. This is the most important thing I can tell you. Only on very rare occasions is it not paid back tenfold. It's not cynical either; this goes a long way to keeping the atmosphere right – my next point, in fact.

- Keep things as **light-hearted** as possible. People work better when they are happy.

- **Don't refuse a request** from an employee unless you have to. If you have to, do so for a reason and give it to them straight.

- Similarly **don't tell fibs**. They're grown ups (presumably) and they'll spot it a mile off. If you have something unpalatable to say, then say it. It is as much a measure of them how they take it. If they think you're a liar then trust and loyalty goes out the window.

- In fact, **be as open as possible** at all times. I don't like to spring surprises on people and I make it clear I expect the favour to be returned.

- **Delegate** or you might as well just get the cheapest people you can find sleeping rough and bark orders at them all day on the assumption that they will get roughly 50% of what you are asking them to do right. If you delegate responsibility and follow the principle of trust through then you will eventually get people who trust their own abilities.

- A **weak leader** is often surprisingly better than a strong leader if the weak leader has good people working under him or her. This is especially true of a strong manager who is overcritical.

Under this influence people seem to collectively freeze and no one can make decisions anymore. Responsibility will then 'bottle-neck' at the manager and things just don't get done. It's a horrible, horrible situation. I once worked for someone like this who was the marketing director of a London department store that wasn't Harrods. She was extremely astute as far as the business went, intelligent and in possession of a powerful personality. Her problem was she assumed people would make the wrong decision at least 90% of the time without her vital input. Sadly I have never seen so much talent wasted and an organisation throw so much money away. By way of illustration, she had around 150 people in her department, most of them graduates, and yet I doubt if any of them did more than three hours' productive work in a day. Instead they spent their time keeping her happy, covering their backs and shifting potential blame.

- **Be yourself**, don't digest the contents of some self-help book and attempt to restructure your personality. The results are almost certainly going to be embarrassing for everyone.

- Don't be afraid of **socialising with staff**. I do it all the time and enjoy it. Most people employ others because they like them, so this shouldn't be a problem in the least. I insist that people take lunch, preferably together, because frankly you will rarely be so busy that taking lunch is not an option. Anyway, if people don't eat for eight hours or take a break they're no good to you or themselves.

- If **people skills** are just not you, hire someone to do it for you. This is the commonest solution to bad management, so don't let it worry you.

Technology

Telling you to keep up-to-date with new technology is stating the obvious. How you do it, though, is important, because keeping up-to-date costs stupid amounts of money if you are not careful. Technology is a time/money thing, and it should save you both. The minute it doesn't fulfil these basic criteria, then you know you are wasting money by buying gadgets you simply don't need. Talking to people you know who work for small companies and large organisations is best. This is done so that you know what your options are and hopefully can at least keep up with the competition. Also, for the same reason that it is important to understand the rules of accounting, so you should understand the principles behind the technology you are using. If you have an in-house 'techie' or hire one in from time to time it stands to reason that there is no way you will know if they are doing a good job if you haven't got the faintest inkling what it is they do in the first place.

Decide on the basics that you need and buy the best.

Nothing slows people down so much or is worse for morale than a dodgy printer or computer that keeps crashing. I have never understood people who employ staff at great expense and then give them a load of old tat to work with. Invariably when a computer crashes the person running it (the crashee, if you will) is likely to involve another member of staff to see if they can help. Let's say that this happens once a day for half an hour:

- Staff costs £15

- Office overhead £5

- Weekly cost £100

Assume that there might be a couple of computers or an out-of-date photocopier or fax and you can quite easily double that figure.

Now bear in mind that a perfectly good new computer can be bought for £200. Calculating the pointless and appalling waste here isn't hard.

In fact, technology is so cheap these days as to make it possible to change all equipment once a year, if you so wish, for relatively little expenditure. And it's worth it from a public image point of view if clients visit your office.

On the morale issue, people love new things and quite rightly feel valued when they are given them. If they are made to work at a cruddy old computer for eight hours a day, they are bound to feel frustrated and unfulfilled at work and more than a little unloved because if you cared enough about them you'd buy them something new once in a while.

Networks

One element that is bound to cause some worry is when you start to build a computer network within the office. Networking should be easy and the benefits are wide ranging, from easy file sharing to monitoring progress of staff across their different functions. As the MD you can dip into the accounts to see the state of the balance sheet, monitor correspondence or just generally be nosey. It's all part of the fun of being the owner.

But networks have a nasty habit of crashing – they all do, even the most expensive – so go for something tried, cheap and tested. Be sure, though, that the person who installs it shows you how to repair basic network crashes (make it part of the requirement). There is nothing so costly as having to get an engineer in just to fix a poor network link. It's really very simple to fix yourself, which means it's like paying £60 to have someone come over and plug your video into your TV.

Remember

The minute you stop understanding the exact nature of the jobs people do for you then you are leaving yourself open to getting ripped off. Also make it your business from here on in to know the costs of things. Once procedure and value are understood,

---

you are in a strong enough position to negotiate and crack the whip.

Knowledge is by far the best and most saleable of commodities because the price attached to it knows no limit, if you happen to know something other people don't. By the same token, if someone suspects you have not got an exact figure placed on the value of what they are being asked by you to do, the price will certainly go up, never down.

Building a Reputation

Practically every sector of the economy has its own 'Guild of This' or 'Association of That' these days.

I'll probably get myself into hot water for saying this but frankly, most of them seem to exist solely to make subscription money out of you. They tend to offer little by way of support and information that you couldn't get for free from the local library or the DBIS. Some may offer professional indemnity insurance at what they claim is a discounted rate. Check this before signing up.

Others claim to offer you professional credibility as they have certain criteria for membership and therefore belonging means that your company performs to certain standards. This is good for some areas where the governing body is well-known (CORGI plumbers, for example) but again check with existing and potential customers whether they know about the association membership or even care whether you belong or not.

There is generally a three-point checklist for testing the potential worth of joining an association, which goes as follows:

1. Will they let you talk with existing members?

2. How quick are they to respond to any queries you may have?

3. Are they run for profit (usually by another company as a sort of side-show to their existing business)? That other company can often also be a competitor.

As well as guilds and associations, networking events are increasingly popular ways of trying to build your business's reputation face-to-face. These include business breakfasts and evening functions where you go along, present your company to 30 or so strangers and then let them do the same. Then you all get a cup of coffee, something to eat, a warm glass of wine (after 5pm) and you try and sell each other things.

Theoretically this should be a nightmare – lots of desperate small business owners meeting at three-star hotels to sell their services to people who have no interest in independent financial services, mobile hairdressing, soft furnishings or acupuncture. However, I've been to about 40 or 50 of these things over the years and the success rate is usually about one good client gained for every ten meetings, which isn't at all bad. If you fix computers for a living, I am told that you can be even more successful.

There are other memberships and associations that are more social than functional and serve your specific industry. These can be good, if you are the type of industry that gets along with one another (they do exist). Sometimes it's nice to be able to moan to people with common ground.

A note on ISO 9000

Set up to replace the old British Standard (BS 9000 numbers) this is an internationally-recognised mark of quality. I suspect the criteria for accreditation have loosened off over the years but it is still undoubtedly the only really well-known accreditation worldwide. Part of the reason for its success is that it concentrates on proper, measurable quality control procedures you have in place for the products or services you provide and it is independently tested once a year.

These criteria do not vary, so everyone is treated the same, hence its wide recognition.

It costs about £1500 for the initial consultations and visits by an examiner to gauge your worthiness for membership, then around another £500 a year to maintain the accreditation. In my experience, it is definitely worth the money if yours is the sort of business where demonstrating quality control to new and existing clients is paramount.

Suppliers

Tricky one, this. Ultimately, if they're any good you need them as much as they need you. The truth of the matter is your dealings with them contain a fair amount of bluff by both parties. Suppliers rarely let on how important your business is to them; they'd be stupid to. By the same token, you rarely let on just how hard they may be to replace.

Many good business people believe strongly in the 'treat them hard, keep their respect' approach. An abrupt manner, suggesting impatience and a bad temper simmering just below the surface is all they think is required most of the time. They cultivate some annoying way of dealing with their suppliers, like only ever by fax, and refuse to return their calls. This establishes the unspoken idea that they do EVERYTHING on their own terms. They never speak to them direct, unless it is to shout about something, and they always get someone else to make their calls first.

This distancing and intimidation tactic is very effective for getting what you want for less than you'd pay elsewhere. If a supplier thinks you are an important person, they will naturally believe your company is a successful one and that your business with them will most likely grow. They can then be intimidated by you in all sorts of ways and this leads to them going the extra mile or so for you.

What can I say? It is effective for suppliers, especially in a competitive market, in the short term.

Unfortunately, for the potential Pol Pots amongst you, this approach is effective usually only in the short term as very few people will put up with this sort of despicable behaviour for long.

If it happens to you, then be polite but make it clear that you won't stand for any nonsense and they usually back down. Don't worry too much about losing business – this sort of business will rarely produce great profits. If it does, you've got to ask yourself where the independent free-spirited business person who had the guts to start out on their own got to? In reality you've just become someone else's employee but without a regular pay cheque.

A better approach with potential suppliers is a more constructive one. State your needs clearly at the outset, and ask them to confirm that they are able to supply what you want in writing. Make sure that they are aware that you are serious about two things:

1. The fact that this is a professional relationship and that it is essentially a financial transaction between professionals in the early stages. Money is two-thirds of your relationship. Professionalism is the rest.

2. If you accord them with respect you expect the compliment to be returned. You have common goals, after all. If they work well for you, your business will thrive and this will mean more work for them. People tend to forget this.

Treat them with politeness at all times; always return their calls. If they work with you a lot, then move onto the next stage: invite them to lunch, take the time to talk to them about matters not related to business. Make sure you are light-hearted whenever the situation allows. They will enjoy, not dread, dealings with you. And consequently everybody will achieve more.

If they do make mistakes or displease you in some way, don't rant down the phone at them. Write formally, immediately, and request an answer by return. The follow-up to this from you should be a phone call to acknowledge their letter and put things back on a friendlier tack. It's a quirk of human nature that the angry person who wrote to them will not be equated with the pleasant person they have always known on the phone, so the air is very easily cleared.

If they do not come back to you in a satisfactory manner it can only be for two reasons:

1. They are lazy and disorganised.

2. Their circumstances have changed and they no longer attach importance to your business.

If you know them very well you may want to give them a second chance. But take care; unless you are positive you can salvage the situation, drop them now. A supplier who starts to go off the boil nearly always only gets worse.

I've been caught out like this several times over the years and I have always regretted continuing to work with an unwilling supplier. They usually end up either producing poor work, neglecting deadlines, overcharging or, very possibly, a combination of all three.

Banks

Like I said earlier, banks tend to ignore you until you have proved your worth to them and yourself. By ignore, I don't mean you can run up huge bills and still expect to get money out of cashpoint machines late on Saturday night. But for the first three years of my existence in business, apart from the occasional request to look at my balance sheet (about once a year), they left me and my £3000 loan metaphorically tucked away in some drawer. After that I decided that it was high time they sat up and took some notice of the Bennett Group and the evil genius behind the controls, so I arranged a meeting.

Ostensibly this was to organise an overdraft facility, though really I wanted to know just what they thought of me. At the time I had an inkling I would need some money for some (cautious) expansion and they were my first port of call. How they viewed the business and its future was important.

Since then I have learnt that banks are very like HMRC, in that if you are straightforward with them they will be the same with you. If not kept in the picture, they have a tendency to panic and withdraw their loans and overdraft facilities, with often disastrous consequences. They can still withdraw their support at any time for reasons that have nothing to do with you. For this reason alone I would never advocate taking out a loan that the business assets cannot cover. If you put your house up as security the bank are likely to go for that every time, before considering other options. Why? Because it is easier to sell a house in practically any market than get a good price for a failing business.

If the bank asks for the house as security on a loan, refuse. It's always seemed like the last desperate act of a person to do this and I would say that to do so is to go in over your head. There should be no need to take risks like this. Golden, once-in-a-lifetime opportunities that might justify such a move for a loan don't exist; there will always be another one.

I have an overdraft facility which I have used only six times in 12 years and for no more than a week each time. Also, I think banks are wise to the trick of borrowing a small sum which you pay off quickly in the hope of going for a big sum shortly after, which you pay off slowly or not at all. Generally, I let them know what we are doing over lunch once every couple of months.

It also pays not to have all your eggs in one basket, as people have seen recently. As a rule of thumb, three banks is enough: one for the business, one personal and one savings.

Clients

As stated earlier with the piece on sales, be yourself. Ongoing client relationships are very much part of the sales process.

Most people make the mistake, early on, of assuming a fictitious alter ego when dealing with people who might be prepared to give them money. And this is only natural; they are important people in your life, after all, and the persona is often as much to disguise nerves as it is to show what you hope is the side of you they would like to buy from.

The brisk, salesy, overconfident approach is irritating and goes no way to establishing a proper rapport with the person you are dealing with. The over-enthusiastic, whatever-you-say-mate approach is equally cloying, unless you are Australian and somehow manage to make it sound sincere. I've also seen people go the other way and end up with an awful personality somewhat like a school matron or bossy older sister. Again, it's usually nerves.

The crux of the issue is that being anything but yourself is a transparent fib. There's a lot bubbling below the surface of human relations and seven parts out of ten, I suspect, is pure instinct. Just as you can spot someone being phoney a mile off, so can the person in whose office you are sitting and whose coffee you are now drinking.

If they feel, even without voicing the thought in their own heads, that you are a fake they may still buy from you but your relationship will always be on a very superficial level and that is not what you want.

People spend most of their days in relationships like this. If someone feels they can relate to you because they feel like they know you on a fairly profound personal level, then you will stand out. And that is what you want to achieve. People buy from you, not just because they need your services and because you supply this (your competitors do too) but because they like you; and they like you because they trust you. Simply put, it is virtually impossible to like or trust someone who is playing up to the role of 'business person'.

Fake clients

These are people to watch for as they are the time wasters. The inveterate, 'yes, come and see me, by all means,' people who really have no intention of buying from you. Instead you serve to flatter their ego. Coming all that way to see them makes them feel important (they get the big chair in the meeting room) and it's fine for them because they're just not that busy. Seeing you gives them the excuse to get out of doing any real work by saying they are seeing suppliers. They'll just use you as an excuse to have an extended coffee break or they'll get you to buy them lunch.

How can you spot the time wasters? The short answer is that it is very hard. But here are a few pointers:

- They agree to your request far too readily, without laying out any agenda for the meeting or without giving you any clear indication whether they really are a company that has a use for what you offer.

- They are not very senior, despite their posturing. They talk vaguely about recommending you to their boss.

- They ask to meet around lunchtime ('say 12-ish').

A note on nerves

If you are of a nervous disposition around important people you've never met before it's perfectly understandable. The only way out of it is habit. Arrange to see as many people as possible, even the fakers, *especially* the fakers. You'll gradually get used to these visits and before you know it you'll be ready for the big meetings without so much as a flicker of emotion.

Trade Fairs and Conferences

These have been part of the business landscape for centuries and no one can really say why. Very few people enjoy them because they're expensive and boring to boot. The commonest way that people contend with them is to get drunk and/or have an affair. Far be it for me to moralise but, let's face it, either way is not going to help your business much, and if you really wanted to get shit-faced and sleep around for kicks, then you could do it without going to Rotterdam or the Holiday Inn just outside Coventry.

Maybe schlepping to Coventry is all part of the excitement but somehow I seriously doubt it.

However, the real problem with conferences and trade fairs is that they're here to stay. If I can draw an analogy, they are like that teenage party you had to go to because all your friends were going. Once there it was all soggy crisps and dodgy punch. But the important thing was that you made it, you showed your face in public and announced your presence in the dating queue.

Likewise with trade fairs, they're the dull part of the corporate dating game, a party you cannot afford to miss, however much you may want to.

There are two sorts of fair:

1. One organised by your own industry so that people visiting get a chance to source all their potential suppliers in one hall.

These are tricky. If all you can afford is a crappy stand next to the ladies' loo, then quite clearly being there is not going to be constructive. Unless you can afford something quite splendid, there's no point in displaying your business.

However, what they are is a very good way of seeing what the competition is up to. Go as a private individual and just walk around. I once went to one of these and left a stack of our brochures by a main entrance when no one was looking. It was one of the most successful fairs I've been to! We got loads of business for the price of a tube ticket and half a morning's low-level industrial espionage.

2. The other type of trade fair is made up of stands full of your potential clients, who are not in your business but who buy from your business.

Again, they are expensive; but again, you don't have to take a stand. For years I used to turn up to these things – as I told clients – because I was 'passing through' and thought I might pop in. Once I'd met up with a few clients I could generally get myself invited to one of the evening launch parties, which was where the real selling went on. I would then spend the next day or so stopping off at stands, chewing the fat with potential clients and pocketing their business cards.

I'll sound a note of caution on this one. You cannot obviously approach someone who is recruited to sell for his or her company and expect them to be remotely interested in you selling to them. If the same happened to you you'd be pretty pissed off. No, the essential thing is to chat about their business to them and then ask them for a card and maybe even take one of their brochures. When they give you their card, (they've just had tons printed specially, so they're keen to get rid of them) offer them yours by way of courtesy. Your card will put you on the mailing list for the marketing department so you can keep up-to-date with what your potential client is doing or striving to achieve (and in this you may be able to help them) and it may even filter through to one of those departments like Human Resources who are often responsible for work being put your way.

Needless to say, though, you now have their brochure, a contact and therefore an excuse to ring them for a pitch. Collect 50 of these in a day and one or two will nearly always pay off.

Also, you don't have to go for the whole three to five days or whatever it is. I usually go for a day or two and leave it at that.

A note on playing with bigger boys

Watch out for this. There are plenty of really good companies who go for one big client and regret it bitterly. I am not here to suggest you turn away business – and life-changing, profitable business at that. However, if you are a one-client company you are obviously in a very difficult position and you should sell your way out of the situation as soon as you can. It is far better to have lots of small clients, none of whom are essential to your business, than one who is so important they can dictate payment terms, prices and even the products or services you supply. Large buyers, such as Tesco or Harrods, have so much power these days they can make or break multi-national brands. Imagine what they could do to you.

I would advise that you never have one client worth more than 20% of your total business if you can help it. If you do, then never, ever let on just how important they are, if only for your own peace of mind.

Useful Websites

www.moneyfacts.co.uk/Savings/articles/who-owns-whom-listings.aspx

List of banks and who owns whom. Invaluable.

www.britishchambers.org.uk

For networking.

www.dell.com

In my opinion, still the best for computers online. Customer service second to none.

www.bni-europe.com

Europe-wide networking.

www.linkedin.com

Pre-eminent online networking for serious business people.

4.

Planning for the Long Term

In which we expand without going bust.

Basic Strategies

- With stability comes a healthy cash flow and confidence. Unless you are very sure that you have reached a sustainable level of turnover, use this to grow. Otherwise you will lose momentum and start to go backwards. Most businesses are relentless, which means you can almost never afford to sit back and think, 'There! It's all set up, watch the money roll in.'

- However, beware of losing sight of your core business – the income stream that has got you to where you are. Too many well-established businesses fail when they become a vanity project for their owners, who branch out into attractive yet unprofitable areas.

- Once you can afford it, always keep around six months' worth of operating costs on deposit as a buffer. Likewise, never be tempted to borrow a sum of more than six months' turnover. Stretching yourself financially is a blight on your quality of life and hardly ever serves its main purpose anyway. You do NOT have to spend money to make it.

- Now is a good time to start to understand the mechanics of a larger business such as company valuation, flotations, selling, partnerships, etc. Even if you have no intention of selling.

Creationists, Expansionists and Caretakers

There are roughly three types of business person: creationists, expansionists and caretakers.

The creationist is adept at starting a business from scratch – taking the initial risks, so to speak – and deriving enjoyment at getting the business on its feet. The expansionist cannot wait to get his or her hands on a fledgling enterprise with potential and broaden its horizons. On the other hand, the caretaker is not much cop at any of these but they do possess the right stuff to recognise when a business is in a safe haven and keep it there. It's not that they lack courage – these types are often the most ruthless when it comes to achieving their goals – and standing still is an illusion. What they are actually doing is taking steps to maintain a good market position in the face of competition and that can be a tough agenda.

With the right mental agility it is possible, nay, essential for the entrepreneur to become *all three* as the situation dictates. The real trick is to know when and how. Much has to do with timing – operating within the market and other forces that are out of your hands. However, you can control the speed of growth to a degree, if you have a reasonable set of rules and stick to them.

I have always opted for keeping each business fairly small in terms of turnover as my general guideline, bringing the caretaker principle into play at a fairly early stage when the business gets to between £100K to £300K turnover.

This tends to work for tertiary industries with between a 50% and 100% margin on services rendered after costs. Again, these types of business are my preferred choice.

The major benefit of keeping a host of small businesses is that none will, at that size, cause you any major headaches. You can certainly afford a few staff to help out and it is easy enough to scale down when times get hard. A business like this is unable to rack up any large debts, and provided you have spread your clients and do not rely too heavily on one or two, creditors defaulting won't pose a serious risk to your health, wealth and happiness.

Two £300K-turnover tertiary businesses, run leanly, really should net you around £150-200K in potential dividends (you pay only 20% tax on these). This is a far cry from the millions promised to you in many books but is quite enough for me.

Speaking personally, I also enjoy the variety. At any one time I might have one idea getting off the ground, and the rest at the expansionist or caretaker stage. It stops me from getting bored. But do not try to support new ideas too heavily with the proceeds from an existing stable business. This is a mistake, because invariably you need the stable business to support you.

Always use the principle of starting small and building slow with any new idea, as outlined in the first chapter. Trying to force a new venture through faster than usual costs a lot of money and is risky because you're not even sure yet how much of a market is really there for you. Impatience, dashed with greed and a light flambé of wishful thinking are, in reality, the downfall of most businesses.

A business that is relatively small is also easy to keep track of from the balance sheet. There are not a large number of complicated elements. A glance at the trading figures once a week will tell you how things are going and whether you need to make many changes to the expenditure to keep it profitable.

It will also help tell you whether it is worth expanding. Even so, expansion can still be tricky and a little daunting. So here are some guidelines for that.

Related Markets

Test the waters of related markets very carefully and ask yourself why you didn't think of trying them in the first place. This is important. If you weren't aware of a potential market because your knowledge of the business arena was limited, then you may well be onto a good thing. If, on the other hand, you were aware of the market, but carefully dismissed it, it may be that it's desperation or boredom that's making you consider it now. Apply the following tests.

- How can I reasonably test the market without damaging my existing business through loss of reputation or neglect?

- Where is the point of no return? Don't flog a dead horse but don't get lily-livered and pull out before you have achieved anything. Go with your instincts on this.

- Cost – factor in your time. This should be small. As a rule of thumb, no more than half the cost of what it was to set up the core business.

- Risks versus benefits. Don't include the benefit that the related market somehow complements your core business. This is usually claptrap – i.e. selling sunglasses does not make you an optician. One business being sort of like another is not complementary. Whether or not each concern increases the turnover of the other is.

In short, too many strings to your bow are not a good thing. If you are the sort of person who has masses of ideas, you must learn to rein yourself in. Only concentrate on those markets you can reasonably spend time on to produce results. Jumping from one idea to another before it gets off the ground is the domain of the very rich or the hopeless dreamers amongst us.

Foreign Markets

Really not that hard, these days. I know a good translation agency too! As with Chapter 1, it is relatively painless from your wallet's point of view to start up a virtual office anywhere in the world. In the US it's incredibly cheap at around £30 a month to have a 24-hour freephone line, office address and fax. It's slightly more expensive in France and Germany at around £50 a month, but still not bad and you can go for a really swanky address.

Test their answering technique. Get your friends to phone up and leave messages; ask them how quickly the phone was answered and the level of courtesy they received.

If you need to sell by phone abroad, get someone in your own country who is bilingual. Do not go through an agency – it will cost you an arm and a leg ('un bras et une jambe,' if you're in France). Rather, phone the local university and ask them to leave a note on the notice board. You get some really good people this way. If you pay them a bit over the average, you'll get all the commitment you could wish for.

I generally opt for native speakers, as people react better to local boys and girls. The reason I don't really go in for hiring people abroad is that agents, or reps who do freelance sales for a number of companies, are usually hopeless. Unless, of course, you pay them a large retainer. Then they are hopeless and expensive.

A note on sales-motivation (domestic and foreign)

Sales needs a constant dialogue between the manager (you, presumably) and the sales person. Discussions about who to target, how to target them, how past conversations have gone with potential clients, and new initiatives are a daily occurrence. Sales is a lonely business, funnily enough. You are talking to lots of people, but much of the time no real human interaction is allowed to develop by the potential client. If you leave a sales

---

person to 'get on with it' alone in a room with a phone, they'll naturally get bored and demotivated. All this nonsense about 'self-starters' in the early 1990s was just a pitiful fib to get people to work on a commission-only basis.

Again, much has been written on the subject of motivating staff. Suffice it to say, with sales staff, if you take a genuine interest in what they do at least two to three times a day, and take every available opportunity to keep things relaxed and amusing, you'll get better work out of them. It's that simple.

Do not worry overly about the cost of phone calls. Cheap calls abroad can be bought for the price of a local UK call now. Time was when the quality of the line on these things was so bad it was like having a conversation with someone who lived down a well. Happily, things have greatly improved.

Translation

At the risk of sounding partisan, once you have decided to expand abroad, look at getting your website translated. Bear in mind that a whopping 70% of people surfing the net have little or no practical understanding of English. That's a huge potential market.

The cost is around £80-£90 per 1000 words. Sites these days are small and usually are not more than about 2000 words. Use the text from your home page as a mailshot, too, or in your brochure so that you don't have to keep getting small pieces translated at high cost.

Currencies

One of the headaches of a foreign client base is the exchange rate issue. If you quote people on a regular basis when going for work, make sure that you review the exchange rates on a regular basis, particularly if you are paying people in a different currency to that in which you are invoicing.

Patents and Trademarks

You may believe you now need to protect your ideas.

The rules on copyright, patents, registered trademarks and suchlike are complex and frightfully dull. Do as much research as you can yourself before engaging the costly services of a patent lawyer or consultant. In principle it may seem easy enough to protect your idea but the laws governing the level of protection afforded, the speed with which this protection can be implemented, and whether it is worldwide or merely local, frequently make it a non-viable option for the small business.

Granted, it may be essential if the value of the business resides in the intellectual property of its product – but there are very few companies like this.

Consider this, too: you will also require the time and the funds to prosecute would-be infringers. This is often where the whole legal quilt unravels. Don't be too quick to protect your name just because you think people won't be imaginative enough to think of their own. People rarely appropriate a name on purpose; and having it on your letterhead and as a registered limited company is often quite enough to deter the casual plagiarist.

Accounting

Some people say that business *is* managing cash flow.

More complicated – now that you've got different currencies, more than one bank account and presumably a higher turnover – is control. Hiring a bookkeeper is one thing; employing that same person to be the last word in telling you the state of your financial affairs can be a mistake, however dedicated they are. You must endeavour to understand what is going on, independently of the figures he or she produces every week. Otherwise you have only their word for it and if they make a mistake you'll end up paying.

I keep a rough record of expenses and income, quietly at home on Saturday mornings, usually by taking the following figures into account:

- profit margin on all work totalled for the month

- less monthly running costs.

This tells me roughly how profitable we are. I also keep a weekly eye on the bank statements to keep me abreast of the all-important 'bottom line' (how much cash I actually have) and I will glance at the list of our outstanding invoices that lets me know if we have too many creditors (people owing us money).

It is not an exact science by any means, but this way I can tell if we may have any future problems (in two to six months, depending on how deep our pockets are). This is very much the opposite of a bookkeeper, who can only reliably tell you what's just happened and possibly what will happen no more than about four weeks in advance.

I can tell a bad month will only show up on our cash flow in about 12 weeks' time. Knowing this is useful, as I can then fully instruct the bookkeeper on how I want the finances and budgets managed over the next few weeks. So make sure you have a firm grasp of how the mechanics of getting paid in your business works; and, by the same token, how often you have to pay expenses prior to this. This gives you a handle on the cash flow like no balance sheet can.

Essentially any figures the bookkeeper comes up with in the next two to three months you should already know about. Their job is far more concerned with the here and now: the balance sheet they are producing tells you how much of the money in the bank is actually yours and how much more you can expect in the short term on what you have invoiced.

For lots of reasons, I have never come across an accounting package that beats looking long and hard at the order book and having a good idea of one's margins and expenses. The figures that pop out of these systems are only as good as the information input. Suppliers have a nasty habit of not sending their bills in soon enough, or you might be slow sending your bills out – either way, these things can make the balance sheet go hopelessly wrong. It's up to you, and you alone, to spot it.

I recommend having a health check done yourself and a balance sheet to go with it, at least once a week. That way you should never be confronted with any nasty surprises.

It is crucial to do a forecast (see the appendix) about once every six months, particularly if you are investing in new staff and your basic business structure is changing.

Useful Websites

www.ipo.gov.uk

Intellectual property office in the UK.

www.yoursmallbusiness.co.uk/how-grow-expand-business.html

Dealing with the expansion of your business.

www.businesslink.gov.uk/bdotg/action/layer?topicId=1073858944

Financial planning.

5.

Reflections

Recommendations for small business ideas and lost causes.

Basic Strategies

- Service industries tend to work best as a small business idea. Particularly the ones where investment in staff and machinery is non-existent to begin with. Take on freelancers on the mutual understanding that you have to get paid before you pay them. This will keep your cash flow positive. But make sure you're upfront with them from the start about this arrangement.

- Selling knowledge beats anything, even property development. Just look at how many consultancies own shiny new office blocks in big cities. They sell advice and there's nothing as notional as that, even insurance.

- If you are creating a high-end brand, don't even attempt it on a budget. It probably won't work. Quality brands take time and lots of cash. Probably better is to aim to play the long game; create an idea that pays the rent and let the brand develop its own identity slowly, like an individual's personality. One day you may wake up to find you have a recognised brand on your hands.

- If you are opening a shop, do it in an area you know well and know your product inside out. How many times have you driven past some new shop in a place you're very familiar with, and without more than a few seconds' reflection, known that it's going to shut down in twelve months? And you're nearly always right.

- No one has ever made money selling homemade 'ethnic' jewellery in flea markets.

- Always trust your instincts and learn to act on them quickly.

Dealing with the Highs

Given what I've been saying throughout most of this book, you may think that the next bit is going to be a homily on not going mad and spending lots of money on things you don't actually need. Quite the opposite. Once you have no debt, a six-month buffer and your turnover is on target, then spend the rest on whatever you want. I generally do. It is very important to be the first to reward yourself when times are good.

And the lows?

What to Do if You Think You Might Fail

This is obviously not a fun place to be but I think that one can safely say it's going to happen to you sooner or later in almost any business. And, as things are always usually hardest at the start, sooner is the more likely scenario. First, if you have followed the advice in this book, you are going to have a very small amount of debt and a reasonably lean operation – ergo, low overheads. The upshot is that there is no reason to give up at this stage. You also have a back-up source of income that should be able to carry you through the worst. Put this into play immediately. The next thing to do is take a critical look at why you are in this situation – not so that you can issue self-recriminations long into the night whilst drowning your sorrows with the Christmas sherry. But try and understand why it's happened, and it's very likely you'll be able to figure out how to get yourself out of this mess. For example, if you are not financially stretched, then the most obvious reason for going bust is lack of sales. Very early in my 'career', I read somewhere that there are three ways to increase sales:

- Drop prices.

- Re-assess the sales and marketing technique.

- Raise prices.

And over the years I've come to see this as more than just a bit of glib advice. My own addition to the above three points is that dropping the price works in the short term, so you need to work out how desperate you are. Putting the price up is very risky but it actually does work if you've got the right market.

However, reassessing the sales and marketing technique is often the only true answer. It might be something very minor, like timid closing (back to the point that people do not like to hear the word 'no'), or it might be something more fundamental, such as your telesales targets not being approachable by phone because reception is doing its job very vigorously. Either way, now is often the time to think and act freely. You have very little to lose, so you can try something outrageous that you suspect may be audacious enough to work. Having fun with something new may not necessarily produce the results you were looking for but it may just turn out to be the shot in the arm that re-invigorates you and, consequently, the business.

Conclusion

One month after my first business started in 1992, my father's own company went from trading relatively well to bust within just five days, over a delayed payment from a supermarket chain and a jittery bank. This does not count the intervening weekend when everybody who worked there nicked half the office furniture and all the best stationery. It left my family, including a live-in grandfather, with an unmanageable debt, the grim reality of the family home being repossessed by the bank and few re-employment prospects for a man in his late fifties.

In the end it took nearly ten years of fighting the bank to save the house and all the furniture inside – interestingly, nearly one-third of the debt with the bank was for insolvency consulting. Funnily enough, those consultants were owned by the bank.

And at exactly the same time my adored girlfriend of over five years ended it with me one miserable Sunday in February on Clapham Common.

With the combined effects of the early '90s recession and my personal misfortunes weighing me down, it now seems rash that I went ahead with business at all.

This book is certainly not about taking stupid risks, but in a sense there was no risk. Although I wasn't earning much, my debt level was very small. Although my confidence was at a low ebb for a bit, I had a burning motivation to turn things around. Looking back, with low overheads and no debt, and a strong reason to be motivated, it would have been very hard to actually fail – provided I was actually trying.

So, I think the point that needs making here is that, although no one said it was going to be easy, it is very rare indeed that you will fail to make things work if you want success enough, and are prepared to work for it.

Good luck!

ROBIN BENNETT
HENLEY-ON-THAMES, 2010

Appendix

A Model Company

In which we see an example of a start-up company that, in a very simple fashion, earns you £50,000 by the end of year one, and £100,000-plus by the end of year two.

We are going to establish a hypothetical recruitment company that specialises in supplying trained technical writers to blue-chip firms.

The USP of the company is that it takes only 10% of first salary (usually the figure is closer to about 15-20%) and that it will initially tailor its services purely towards supplying the automotive industry. Just so as nobody is in any doubt, we will call it Automotive Copywrite Ltd.

The benefit of a recruitment consultancy supplying only full-time staff is that the overheads are very low. It's my favourite kind of enterprise. The start-up costs are non-existent – all you need is a phone, a computer, an internet connection and a good website. Sourcing good staff is key and this can be done online through specialist recruitment sites. Pick a couple and the subscription cost will be around £100 a month. A technical writer will get between £25,000 and £40,000 a year, according to field and experience. This averages out at, say, £3000 a placement. Our target is to get one placement in the first two months and then pick up the pace to around three a month in the first year and ten a month by the end of year two, once we decide we are up to diversifying our client base somewhat. This target is very achievable, with no more than one or two staff.

Clients will pay on presentation of invoice within 14 days, if you are insistent on two things:

1. Firstly that you are giving them a whopping 25% discount.

2. Secondly, if the placement does not work out in the first 60 days, they get their money back. In full.

Getting paid in 14 days means that you have pretty much 45 working days to find a client willing to give you a try, find a candidate and get them into work. Again, this is fairly achievable – the prospective client will have nothing to lose getting you to look for them, as it is not costing them anything and you are cheaper than anyone else.

Now the way that a basic cash flow forecast works is quite simply as follows: it takes your income for the month and totals it. Then it takes your expenses for the month and totals them. Whatever is left as profit, or owing, you carry over to the next month. And so on. It is based on a projected income – hence the forecast bit. And the flow of money into and out of your trading account – hence the flow bit. So, for example, in month one, our income is only the loan, £5000 and the expenses totalling £2600, leaving a positive balance of £2400 left in the piggy bank. In month two, when we get our first small commission, we finish up with £2150.

Assuming that by month six we finally manage to pull off a payment for two placements in a month we have put enough by to pay back the loan if we wish, plus interest. By month 12, if we are getting three placements, then by the end of year we have £15,400 in our account, so we can pay ourselves a bonus of £10,000 on top of our first year's salary of 40-odd thousand and re-invest the rest in the business.

In year two, you may decide to carry on as you were at the end of year one – after all, you've paid yourself a good salary and bonus and you really don't need any staff to run this size of enterprise. However, if you want to grow, allow for an expensive month 13 and 17. If the staff work well, set a target of three people, including yourself, generating three to four placements a month each – £30,000 and a nice big bonus of £40,000 on a salary of £90,000.

Now you can finally stop worrying about the mortgage. These figures are not made up. Year two is very similar to the accounts for one of my businesses last year, which is run with only three part-time staff and in a similar field – specialist recruitment.

PAYE and bonuses

Barring PAYE (Pay As You Earn), a nice fat bonus is probably the most tax-efficient and least dodgy way to pay yourself. Nonetheless, a bonus can only be paid on profits and any directors must all get an equal share. The current tax rate is 20%. I tend to pay myself a mixture of both but it's really a matter for you to decide with your accountant.

INCOME (Year 1)

MONTH	1	2	3	4	5	6	7	8	9	10	11	12
Sales (£)	0	2,500	3,500	4,500	5,000	6,000	6,000	6,500	7,000	7,500	8,000	9,000
Loan (£)	5,000											
Gross income (£)	5,000	2,500	3,500	4,500	5,000	6,000	6,000	6,500	7,000	7,500	8,000	9,000
Total turnover for year (£)												70,500

INCOME (Year 2)

MONTH	13	14	15	16	17	18	19	20	21	22	23	24
Sales (£)	10,000	11,000	12,000	13,000	14,000	16,000	18,000	20,000	22,000	25,000	27,000	30,000
Loan (£)												
Gross income (£)	10,000	11,000	12,000	13,000	14,000	16,000	18,000	20,000	22,000	25,000	27,000	30,000
Total turnover for year (£)												218,000

EXPENSES (Year 1)

MONTH	1	2	3	4	5	6	7	8	9	10	11	12
Director's salary (£)	1,000	2,000	3,000	3,000	3,000	3,000	3,500	3,500	4,000	4,500	5,000	5,500
Bonus (£)												
Staff salary (£)												
Sourcing (£)	200	200	200	200	200	200	200	200	200	200	200	200
Print (£)	100	100	100	100	100	100	100	100	100	100	100	100
Tel (£)	150	150	150	150	150	150	150	150	150	150	150	150
Travel (£)	300	50	50	50	50	300	300	300	300	300	300	300
Post (£)	150	150	150	150	150	150	150	150	150	150	150	150
Miscellaneous (£)	100	100	100	100	100	100	100	100	100	100	100	100
Rent (£)												
Equipment (£)	500											
Accountancy fees (£)	100											
Total expenses (£)	2,600	2,750	3,750	3,750	3,750	4,000	4,500	4,500	5,000	5,500	6,000	6,500

EXPENSES (Year 2)

MONTH	13	14	15	16	17	18	19	20	21	22	23	24
Director's salary (£)	6,000	6,500	6,500	7,000	7,500	7,500	8,000	8,500	9,000	9,000	9,500	10,000
Bonus (£)	10,000											
Staff salary (£)	1,500	1,500	1,500	1,500	3,500	3,500	3,500	3,500	3,500	3,500	3,500	1,500
Sourcing (£)	400	400	400	400	400	400	400	400	400	400	400	400
Print (£)	200	200	200	200	200	200	200	200	200	200	200	200
Tel (£)	200	200	250	250	250	250	250	250	250	250	250	250
Travel (£)	300	300	300	300	300	300	300	500	600	600	600	600
Post (£)	200	200	200	200	200	200	250	250	250	250	250	250
Miscellaneous (£)	200	200	200	200	200	200	200	200	200	200	200	200
Rent (£)	800	800	800	800	800	800	800	800	800	800	800	800
Equipment (£)	1,000											
Accountancy fees (£)	1,000											
Total expenses (£)	21,800	10,300	10,350	10,850	13,350	13,350	13,900	14,600	15,200	15,200	15,700	14,200

BALANCE SHEET (Year 1)

MONTH	1	2	3	4	5	6	7	8	9	10	11	12
Bank balance start month (£)	5,000	2,400	2,150	1,900	2,650	3,900	5,900	7,400	9,400	11,400	13,400	15,400
Bank balance end month (£)	2,400	2,150	1,900	2,650	3,900	5,900	7,400	9,400	11,400	13,400	15,400	17,900

BALANCE SHEET (Year 2)

MONTH	13	14	15	16	17	18	19	20	21	22	23	24
Bank balance start month (£)	17,900	6,100	6,800	8,450	10,600	11,250	13,900	18,000	23,400	30,200	40,000	51,300
Bank balance end month (£)	6,100	6,800	8,450	10,600	11,250	13,900	18,000	23,400	30,200	40,000	51,300	67,100

Dummy simplified balance sheet

Date	12.12.06
Bank statement (£)	9000
Salaries (£)	-5000
VAT exposure (£)	-2000
Misc expenses (£)	-1000
	1000

CLIENT	Date	Profit (£)	FULL INV. AMOUNT (£)
Red and Co.	1.12.06	340	1,000.00
Derby Ltd	28.11.06	950	2,653.00
Peoples Ltd	20.11.06	4,512	12,655.00
Centre Point Plus	15.11.06	3,215	11,252.00
		9,017	

Total cash in 4-6 weeks: £10,017

Notes

The simplified balance sheet takes the bank statement from 12 December 2006 and subtracts the total expenses for the next four weeks, including money owed to VAT and tax.

Quite simply, it then adds up the total of all invoices due now or in the next four weeks and comes up with a figure which is the total cash which should be in the company bank account in the next four to six weeks, allowing time for late payments. This shows a balance of £10,017, about a 10% growth on the previous month.

Your Business Plan Notes and Ideas

(See pp.12-20 for more details.)

Executive summary

Attention grabber – selling your business; its capital needed and growth expected

Market overview

Overview of the market place and justification for your business

Objectives and strategy

Taking advantage of the market place

Modus operandi

How the business will operate

Structure

Who's running things, what qualifies them; and legal structure

Schedules

What to expect of business progress

Cash flow forecast and notes

Spreadsheet of income, outgoings and bottom line (profit), based on reasonable explanations

Appendices

Case studies and assorted extras

Index

The *Start-Up Smart* Competition

Sometimes we have a good idea but we need just a nudge in the right direction to get us going. The *Start-Up Smart* Competition is hopefully that nudge, and if winning it provides five businesses with the impetus to go out and succeed, then it has been worth it. Especially if those businesses go on to inspire five more budding entrepreneurs each and in turn they each do the same. And so on…

For that reason, I'm running a contest to find the would-be entrepreneurs with the best start-up ideas in the UK that cost £5000 or less to get going – in five categories, with five prizes, to help the winners on their way to success.

The competition is open to anyone living in the United Kingdom between 18-30 years old. No one business should cost more than £5000 in initial set up costs. There will be five winners announced in November 2010 in five categories:

1. Services
2. Manufacturing
3. IT
4. Media and arts
5. Retail

Each prize will award the winner:

- Set-up costs, including help approaching investors or direct funding from Robin Bennett.

- Professional planning to get the company off the ground on the right footing from the start.

- One year's mentoring from Robin Bennett, hands-on support whenever required and access to business networking.

- National and regional PR for the start-up business.

- Substantial marketing on the site www.startupsmart.co.uk.

Initial submissions

Initial submissions can be emailed or sent as a Word file attachment or even as a video file! As a minimum, the applicant is required to set out their business idea in not more than 250 words. We would also like to know a bit about you and roughly how much you think the company would cost to set up and run in its first year (not more than £5000).

Competition entry

The competition is open from 1 June 2010 and last date for entry is 31 October 2010.

Shortlist

A shortlist will be published on 5 November 2010 and those on the shortlist will be asked to provide more detailed information about their background and business idea.

Winners

Five winners will be announced at the end of November 2010.

How to Enter

Email and video submissions

Email us at:

competition@startupsmart.co.uk

(not more than 250 words)

or

Send us a link to a video describing your idea!

The author and publishers reserve the right to use all applicants' entries for purposes of information or marketing.

Other great business titles from

Harriman House

**Small Business
Tax Planning**
*All you need to know
from start-up to
retirement*
Russell Cockburn

9781906659394

Working 5 to 9
*How to start a
successful business in
your spare time*

Emma Jones

9781906659684

**100 Rules for
Entrepreneurs**
*Real-life Business
Lessons*

Neil Lewis

9780857190277

**The New Rules of
Business**
*Leading entrepreneurs
reveal their secrets for
success*

Dan Matthews
9781906659165

Eyewitness
*The Inside Story of a
Publishing
Phenomenon*

Christopher Davis
9781906659196

**The eBay Business
Handbook (3rd
edition)**
*How anyone can build
a business and make
money on eBay.co.uk*
Robert Pugh
9781906659974

 Harriman House